The Glory of Christ

The Glory of Christ

An easier-to-read and abridged version of the classic
'Meditations on the Glory of Christ'
by John Owen, first published in 1684

Prepared by Hervey Mockford

General Editor: J. K. Davies, B.D., Th.D.

© GRACE PUBLICATIONS TRUST
139 Grosvenor Avenue,
London, N5 2NH,
England.

1987

ISBN 0 946462 13 5

Distributed by:

EVANGELICAL PRESS,
16—18 High Street,
Welwyn,
Hertfordshire, AL6 9EQ,
England.

Scripture quotations are from:
The Holy Bible — Revised Authorised Version
(New King James Version)

Cover design by
Mark Prescott — the
flower of the Iris.

Typeset by Inset, Chappel, Essex.
Printed and bound in Great Britain by
Anchor Brendon, Tiptree, Essex.

Contents

Preface

The purpose of this book is to tell how the Bible
describes the glory of our Lord Jesus Christ. His glory
is far too great for our small minds to understand so
we can never give him the praise due to him. But by
faith we can have some knowledge of Christ and his
glory, and that knowledge is better than any other
form of wisdom or understanding. The apostle Paul
said: "I also count all things loss for the excellence
of the knowledge of Christ Jesus my Lord" (Philippians 3:8). If our future happiness means being where
Christ is and seeing his glory, there is no better
preparation for it than to fill our thoughts with that
glory now. So we shall gradually be changed into
that glory.

It is only about Christ that we may boast and glory,
for the following reasons:

1. Our human nature was first made in Adam and
Eve in the image of God, full of beauty and glory.
But sin brought this glory down to the dust and human
nature became completely unlike God, whose image
it had now lost. Satan took control and if left in this
state mankind would have perished eternally. But the
Lord Christ, the Son of God, stooped down in great
pity and love to take human nature to be his own.
So our human nature, after sinking to the lowest depths
of misery, has now been raised above the whole creation

of God. For God has now set Christ at his own right hand in the heavenly places, far above all principality and power and might and dominion and every name that is named, not only in this world but also in that which is to come (Ephesians 1:20, 21). Those who have received faith and grace rightly to understand the purpose of human nature must rejoice that it has been raised from sinful depths into the glory it has now received by the honour given to Christ.

2. In Christ the relationship of our nature to God is always the same. Our original friendship with God at the creation was soon broken by the fall of man. Human beings became God's enemies. But the wisdom and grace of God planned to make our nature once more like his, and to do it in such a way as to make any future separation between us and him impossible. We cannot stop wondering that our nature is capable of sharing the glorious life of God. Almighty wisdom, power and goodness made this possible by Jesus Christ. This work of God is part of the mystery of godliness which angels desire to look into (I Peter 1:12). How sinful and foolish we are if we think too much of other things and not enough of this! The great love of God for mankind is shown by the fact that the Son of God did not come to this earth as an angel but became the man Christ Jesus, having the same nature as ourselves.

3. Christ has shown that it is possible for our human nature to live in heaven. Our minds cannot begin to grasp the numbers and distances of the stars in the sky. How then do we suppose that human beings could live in a heaven more glorious than the skies? Yet our nature, in the man Christ Jesus, has gone to the eternal heaven of light and glory and he has promised that where he is we shall be for ever.

Temptations, trials, sorrows, dangers, fears and sicknesses are all part of this present life. All our concerns have trouble and sorrow in them. But by considering the glory of Christ which we shall share we can obtain relief from all these evils and gain victory over them. "We are hard pressed on every side, yet not crushed; we are perplexed, but not in despair; persecuted, but not forsaken; struck down, but not destroyed. Therefore we do not lose heart. Even though our outward man is perishing, yet the inward man is being renewed day by day. For our light affliction, which is but for a moment, is working for us a far more exceeding and eternal weight of glory, while we do not look at the things which are seen, but at the things which are not seen. For the things which are seen are temporary, but the things which are not seen are eternal" (II Corinthians 4:8, 9, 16—18). What are all the things of this life, either good or evil, compared with the benefit to us of the excellent glory of Christ?

The state of our minds often causes us the greatest trouble. The Psalmist asked himself: "Why are you cast down, O my soul? and why are you disquieted within me?" (Psalm 42:5, 11). The centering of our thoughts by faith on the glory of Christ will bring peace and quiet to the disturbed and disordered mind. It is by Christ that "we have access by faith into this grace in which we stand, and rejoice in hope of the glory of God . . . because the love of God has been poured out in our hearts by the Holy Spirit who was given to us" (Romans 5:2—5).

We may even think cheerfully of death as we fix our thoughts on the glory of Christ. Many live in fear of death all their days. How can we overcome these fears?

1. We must deliberately commit our departing souls into the hand of him who is able to receive and keep them. The soul must alone, by itself, go into eternity.

3

It leaves behind, for ever, everything known before by its own natural senses.

There must, therefore, be an act of faith in giving up the soul to the disposal of God, as Paul was able to do. "I know whom I have believed and am persuaded that he is able to keep what I have committed to him until that day" (II Timothy 1:12). The Lord Jesus Christ is our great example. When he dismissed his spirit, he left his soul in the hand of God his Father, in full assurance that it would come to no evil. "Therefore my heart is glad and . . . my flesh also will rest in hope. For you will not leave my soul in Sheol, nor will you allow your Holy One to see corruption" (Psalm 16:9, 10). The last victorious act of faith takes place at death. The soul says to itself: "You are now leaving time and entering into those eternal things which the natural eye has not seen, nor the ear heard, nor has man's heart been fully able to imagine. Therefore with quietness and confidence give yourself up to the sovereign power, grace, truth and faithfulness of God, and you will find rest and peace". Jesus Christ immediately receives the souls of those who believe in him, as we see in the case of Stephen. When he died, he said: "Lord Jesus, receive my spirit" (Acts 7:59). What can be a greater encouragement to commit our souls into Christ's hands at death than to know every day of our lives something of his glory, his power and his grace?

2. As human beings, we are not like the angels who are pure spirits and cannot die. Nor are we like the animals which have no everlasting soul. But God has designed for us a glorious resurrection body which will no longer have a physical nature: we shall be more like the angels. In this life there is such a close relationship between the soul and body that we try to put out of our minds all thought of their separation from each other. How is it possible, then, to have

such a readiness to die as the apostle Paul, when he said I have "a desire to depart and be with Christ, which is far better" (Philippians 1:23)? Such readiness can only be found by looking by faith at Christ and his glory, and being sure that to be with him is better than this life.

If we want to die cheerfully, we must think how God will call us from the dust of the grave at the resurrection. He will then, by his almighty power, not only restore to us the glory of Adam and Eve at the creation but will add rich blessings beyond our imagination. Let us also remember that although the soul and body of our glorious Saviour were separated at death (in just the same way as ours will be), he now possesses great glory. His example can give us hope.

3. There must be a readiness to accept God's time for us to die. We may, like Moses, wish to see more of the glorious work of God for his people on this earth. Or, like Paul, we may feel it needful for the welfare of others that we should live a little longer. It may be we would like to see our families and personal concerns in a better and more settled state. But we cannot enjoy peace in this world unless we are ready to yield to the will of God in respect of death. Our times are in his hand, at his sovereign disposal. We must accept that as best.

4. Some may not fear death but may dread the way they might die. Long illness, great pain, or some form of violence could be the means of bringing our earthly life to an end. We shall be wise if we are always ready for any experience which God may allow us to pass through. Is it not right that he should do what he will with his own? Is not his will infinitely holy, wise, just and good in all things? Does he not know what is best for us and what will bring most glory to himself? Very many people have found they have

5

been able to endure the things they have dreaded most because much more strength and peace of mind have been given them than they could ever have expected.

But none of these four things can we do, unless we now believe in and enjoy the excellent glory of Christ.

Many more advantages of meditating on the glory of Christ could be said, but my weakness and the approach of death forbid my writing here in more detail.[1]

Reference

1. This book was the last to be written by John Owen, who died in 1683. It was being printed as he died and was published in 1684. These facts give a special significance to this book. Chapters 15 and 16 were not, in fact, printed with the first edition of the book. These two chapters (in Owen's handwriting) were not found until after the first printing. They have been added to subsequent editions of the book and so are included here also.

1.
"That they may behold my glory"
(John 17:24)

The high priest of the Old Testament, having made the required sacrifices on the Day of Atonement, went into the holy place with his hands full of sweet-smelling incense which he put on the fire before the Lord. So the great high priest of the church, our Lord Jesus Christ, having sacrificed himself for our sins, entered into heaven with the sweet perfume of his prayers for his people. His eternal desire for the salvation of his people is shown in the verse quoted above: "that they may behold my glory". Joseph asked his brothers to tell his father of all his glory in Egypt (see Genesis 45:13), not to make a proud show of that glory but to give his father the joy of knowing his high position in the land. So Christ desired his disciples to see his glory that they might be satisfied and enjoy the fulness of his blessing for ever.

Once having known the love of Christ, the heart of the believer will always be restless until the glory of Christ is seen. The climax of all Christ's other requests for his disciples is that they may behold his glory. So I assert that one of the greatest benefits for a believer in this world and the next is to consider the glory of Christ.

Ever since the name of Christian was known on the earth, there has never been such direct opposition to the uniqueness and glory of Christ as at the present day.[1] It is the duty of all those who love the Lord Jesus to testify according to their ability to his uniqueness[2] and glory. I would therefore try to strengthen the faith of true believers by showing that to see the glory of Christ is one of the greatest experiences and privileges possible in this world or the next. Here in this life, beholding the glory of the Lord, they are changed into its likeness (see II Corinthians 3:18). Hereafter, they will be like him for they will see him as he is (see I John 3:2). This knowledge of Christ is the continual life and reward of our souls. He that has seen Christ has seen the Father; the light of the knowledge of the glory of God is seen only in the face of Jesus Christ (see John 14:9; II Corinthians 4:6).

There are two ways of seeing the glory of Christ: by faith, in this world; and by sight, in heaven for eternity. It is the second way that is mainly referred to in our Saviour's prayer — that his disciples may be where he is, to behold his glory. But the view of his glory by faith in this world is also included and I give the following reasons for emphasising this:

1. No man will ever see the glory of Christ hereafter if he does not have some view of it by faith now. We must be prepared by grace for glory and by faith for sight. Some people, who have no real faith, imagine they will see the glory of Christ in heaven but they are deceiving themselves. The apostles saw his glory, "the glory as of the only begotten of the Father, full of grace and truth" (John 1:14). This was not a worldly glory like that of kings or the Pope. Though he made all things, Christ had nowhere to lay his head. There was no unusual glory or beauty in his appearance as a man. His face and form became more disfigured than any man (see Isaiah 52:14; 53:2). Nor could the full glory of his divine nature be seen in this world. How

then did the apostles see his glory? It was by the spiritual understanding of faith. As they saw how full of grace and truth he was in what he did and how he spoke, they "received him and believed on his name" (John 1:12). Those without such faith saw no glory in Christ.

2. The glory of Christ is far beyond the grasp of our present human understanding. We cannot look directly at the sun without being blinded. And with our natural eyes we cannot have any true view of the glory of Christ in heaven; it can only be known by faith. Those who talk or write about the immortality of the soul but have no knowledge of the life of faith can have no conviction in what they say. There are those, too, who use images, pictures and music in a vain attempt to help them worship something they imagine is like the glory of God. This is only because they have no spiritual understanding of the true glory of Christ. The understanding that only comes by faith will give us a true idea of Christ's glory and create desires for its full enjoyment.

3. If, therefore, we would have a more active faith and a greater love to Christ, giving rest and satisfaction to our souls, we must seek to have a greater desire to see more of his glory in this life. This will mean that the things of this world will have less and less attraction for us until they become as undesirable as something dead. We should not look for anything in heaven other than what we have some experience of in this life. If we were fully persuaded of this we would be more often thinking about heavenly things than we usually are.

Before I try to lead believers into the more personal experiences of faith, love and holy meditation, I will mention some of the advantages arising from constantly thinking about the glory of Christ by faith.

1. We shall be made fit for heaven. Many think themselves already fit enough for glory, if they could reach it. But they do not know what it is. There is no pleasure in music for the deaf, nor in the most beautiful colours for the blind. So heaven would be no pleasure to persons who have not been prepared for it in this life by the Spirit. The apostle gives "thanks to the Father who has qualified us to be partakers of the inheritance of the saints in the light" (Colossians 1:12). The will of God is that we should know the beginning of glory here and its fulness hereafter. But we are made capable of receiving the knowledge of this glory by the spiritual activity of faith. Our present knowledge of glory is our preparation for future glory.

2. A true view of Christ's glory has the power to change us until we become like Christ (see II Corinthians 3:18).

3. Regular meditation on the glory of Christ will give rest and satisfaction to our souls. It will bring peace to our minds which are so often filled with fears and disturbing thoughts. For "to be spiritually minded is life and peace" (Romans 8:6). The things of this life are nothing when compared with the great value and beauty of Christ, as Paul said: "I also count all things loss for the excellence of the knowledge of Christ Jesus my Lord" (Philippians 3:8).

4. Knowledge of the glory of Christ is the source of our everlasting blessedness. By seeing him as he is, we shall be made like him (see I Thessalonians 4:17; John 17:24; I John 3:2).

God is so great that we cannot see him with our natural eyes and even when in heaven we shall not be able to understand everything about him, for he is infinite. The blessed sight we shall there have of God will always be "in the face of Jesus Christ" (II Corinthians 4:6) and this will be enough to fill us with peace and a sense of rest and glory.

10

Yet even in this life true believers sometimes have a little experience of the pleasure to be found in knowing Christ. The scriptures and the Holy Spirit bring such a sense of the uncreated glory of God shining in Christ that it fills their souls with indescribable joy and peace. These experiences are not frequent but that is because of our idleness and lack of spiritual light. Glory would dawn in our souls more often if we were diligent in our duty of meditating on the glory of Christ.

In chapters two to eleven I will try to answer the question: "What is the glory of Christ that we may behold by faith, and how do we see it?" And in chapters twelve to fourteen: "How does the knowledge of faith differ from the immediate sight of Christ in heaven?"

References
1. i.e. 1683.
2. See chapter three where this uniqueness is described in detail.

2.
The glory of Christ as the only representative of God to believers

The glory of God arises from his holy nature and from the excellent things he does. But we can only see this glory by looking at Jesus Christ (II Corinthians 4:6). Christ is "the brightness of the Father's glory" and "the image of the invisible God" (Hebrews 1:3; Colossians 1:15). He shows us the glorious nature of God and reveals his will for us. Without Christ, we should never see God at any time, either here or hereafter (see John 1:18). He and the Father are one. When Christ became a man he displayed the glory of his Father. He alone makes known to angels and human beings the glory of the invisible God. This revelation is the rock on which the church is built, the ground of all our hopes of salvation and eternal life. Those who cannot see this glory of Christ by faith do not know God. They are like the unbelieving Jews and Gentiles of old. "For Jews request a sign, and Greeks seek after wisdom; but we preach Christ crucified, to the Jews a stumbling-block and to the Greeks foolishness, but to those who are called, both Jews and Greeks, Christ the power of God and the wisdom of God" (I Corinthians 1:22—24).

Ever since the preaching of the gospel began, the devil's great purpose has been to blind people's eyes to the glory of Christ. "If our gospel is veiled, it is veiled to those who are perishing, whose minds the god of this age has blinded, who do not believe, lest the light of the gospel of the glory of Christ, who is the image of God, should shine on them" (II Corinthians 4:3, 4). This blindness, or darkness, is cured in those who believe by the mighty power of God. "For it is the God who commanded light to shine out of darkness who has shone in our hearts to give the light of the knowledge of the glory of God in the face of Jesus Christ" (II Corinthians 4:6).

A great part of the misery and punishment of humanity because of Adam's fall into sin has been the thick darkness and ignorance which has covered the human mind since that time. Men and women have boasted that they were wise, but their wisdom did not bring them to God (see I Corinthians 1:21; Romans 1:21). The reasoning of philosophers about things that are invisible and beyond human understanding does not save people from idolatry and the practice of all kinds of sin. Satan is the prince of darkness and he set up his kingdom of darkness in human minds, keeping them in ignorance of God. All wickedness and confusion among human beings come from this darkness, this ignorance of God. God might have left us to perish in the blindness and ignorance of our ancestors but he has brought us "out of darkness into his marvellous light" (I Peter 2:9). The special glory and privilege of Israel were the words of God. "He declares his word to Jacob, his statutes and his judgments to Israel. He has not dealt thus with any nation" (Psalm 147:19, 20). Yet God spoke to them from thick darkness because they could not understand the glory which was later to be made known by Christ. When Christ came, it was seen that "God is light, and in him is no darkness at all" (I John 1:5). When the Son of God appeared in human flesh, God showed that the divine nature was a glorious nature of three persons in one — a Trinity. The light of this knowledge shone into the darkness in the world so

13

that no-one could continue to be ignorant of God except those who would not see (see John 1:5, 14, 17, 18; II Corinthians 4:3, 4). The glory of Christ is that he reveals this truth about the invisible nature of God.

When we first believe, we see God the Father in Christ. We have no need of Philip's request: "Lord, show us the Father", because having seen Christ by faith, we have seen the Father also (John 14:8, 9). David longed for this view. "O God, you are my God; early will I seek you; my soul thirsts for you, my flesh longs for you . . . so I have looked for you in the sanctuary, to see your power and your glory." (Psalm 63:1, 2). In the tabernacle there was only a very obscure representation of the glory of God. How much more should we value the view we may have of it, though still "as in a glass" (II Corinthians 3:18)? Moses had seen many wonderful works of God but he knew that the real satisfaction of soul was in seeing the glory of God. So he prays: "Please, show me your glory" (Exodus 33:18). It is in Christ alone that we may have a clear, distinct view of the glory of God and his excellencies.

Infinite wisdom is part of the divine nature and is the source of all the glorious works of God. "But where can wisdom be found?" (Job 28:12). We can see wisdom by its effects, among the greatest of which is the salvation of the Church. The apostle Paul was called "to make all people see what is the fellowship of the mystery, which from the beginning of the ages has been hidden in God who created all things through Jesus Christ; to the intent that now the manifold wisdom of God might be made known by the church, to the principalities and powers in the heavenly places" (Ephesians 3:9, 10). The divine wisdom shown in the created world around us, great as it is, is little compared with the wisdom of God made known to us in Christ

Jesus. But only believers see the wisdom of God in Christ; it is not seen by unbelievers (see I Corinthians 1:22—24). If we are wise enough to see this wisdom clearly, we shall have "joy inexpressible and full of glory" (I Peter 1:8).

We must also consider the love of God as part of the divine nature, "for God is love" (I John 4:8). The best ideas of men are imperfect and affected by sin. They think that God is easy-going, one who is just like themselves (see Psalm 50:21). Those who do not know Christ do not realise that although God is love, his wrath "is revealed from heaven against all ungodliness and unrighteousness of men" (Romans 1:18). How then shall we know the love of God and see his glory in it? The apostle tells us: "In this the love of God was manifested toward us, that God has sent his only begotten Son into the world, that we might live through him" (I John 4:9). This is the only evidence given to us that God is love. We should still be in complete darkness if the Son of God had not come to show us the true nature and activity of divine love. Here we see how beautiful, glorious and desirable Christ is, as the one who shows that God is love.

To see this glory is the only way of our obtaining holiness, comfort and preparation for eternal glory. Consider therefore what God has made known about himself in his Son, especially his wisdom, love, goodness, grace and mercy. The life of our souls depends on these things. As the Lord Christ is the only appointed way to these blessings, how exceedingly glorious he must be in the eyes of believers!

There are some who look on Christ as a great teacher but not as the unique expression of the invisible God. But if you have a desire for heavenly things, I ask: "Why do you love and trust Jesus Christ? Can you give a reason for the hope that is in you? Is one reason because you see the glory of God in bringing about, through Christ, the blessings of salvation which otherwise would have been eternally hidden from you?" There is a promise that in New Testament days our "eyes will see the king in his beauty" (Isaiah 33:17). What is this beauty of Christ? It is that God is in him and so he is the great representative of the glory of God to us. Who can describe the glory of this privilege, that we who were born in darkness and deserved to be cast into utter darkness should be brought into this marvellous "light of the knowledge of the glory of God in the face of Jesus Christ" (II Corinthians 4:6)?

Unbelief blinds the eyes of people's minds. Even among those who say they have a knowledge of Christ, there are only a few who understand his glory and who are changed into his likeness. No one will ever become like Christ simply by imitating his actions. Only an experience of Christ's glory has the power to make a believer Christlike. The truth is that the best of us is unwilling to spend time in serious thought on this subject. Thoughts of the glory of Christ are too high and too hard for us. We cannot delight in them for very long without becoming weary and turning away from them. We are unspiritual, our thoughts and desires being taken up with other things. If we would stir ourselves to believe "the things the angels desire to look into", our spiritual understanding and strength would increase daily. We would then show more of the glory of Christ by the way we live and death itself would be welcome to us!

There are those who say they do not understand these things. In any case, they say, such understanding is not necessary for us to live practical Christian lives. My answer to this objection is as follows:

1. There is nothing more fully and clearly revealed in the gospel than that Jesus Christ is the expression of

the invisible God, so that in seeing him we see the Father also. If this essential truth is not received and believed, all other Bible truths are useless to our souls. The whole gospel is turned into a fable if we accept Christ as merely a great teacher and do not accept the truth of his unique character.[1]

2. The chief reason why faith is given us is in order that we may see the glory of God in Christ and meditate on all its effects. If we do not have this understanding, which is given by the power of God to those who believe, we shall not know anything of the whole mystery of the gospel (see Ephesians 1:17–19; II Corinthians 4:3–6).

3. Christ is infinitely glorious, above the whole creation, because only through him is the glory of the invisible God made most fully known to us and by him alone the image of God is renewed in us.

4. Faith in Christ as the one who reveals the glory of God is the root from which all Christian practice grows. Anyone who does not possess this kind of faith cannot be a true Christian.

To those who find this teaching about faith a little strange but would like to know more, I give the following advice:

i. The greatest privilege in this life is to see the glory of God the Father in all his holiness displayed in Christ. For this is life eternal, to know the Father, the only true God, and Jesus Christ whom he has sent (see John 17:3). Unless you value this as a great privilege, you will not enjoy it.

ii. Knowledge of Christ is a great mystery which requires much spiritual wisdom to understand and to make of practical value. Human reasoning will not help us at all; we must be taught by God himself (see John 1:12, 13; Matthew 16:16, 17). As a craftsman has to

17

train himself in the skills of his trade, so must we use the ways appointed by God for the purpose of making us skilled believers. The chief of these ways is earnest prayer. Pray like Moses that God would show you his glory. Pray like Paul, "that the God of our Lord Jesus Christ, the Father of glory, may give you the spirit of wisdom and revelation in the knowledge of him" (Ephesians 1:17). Lazy souls never obtain any experience of this glory but to seek it by the ways God commands is pleasant.

iii. Learn from the ungodly — how earnestly they pursue their sinful desires and continually meditate on them. Shall we be lazy in meditating on that glory which we hope one day to see more fully?

iv. The heavens declare the glory of God but we learn there little about the glory of God compared with the knowledge of it given to us in Christ Jesus. The cleverest people and greatest thinkers are blind compared with those who are least in the kingdom of heaven but who know the glory of Christ.

What we should really desire, then, is to know the power of this truth in our hearts. Do we want to have the same joy, rest, delight and indescribable satisfaction as the saints above? Our present knowledge of the glory of Christ is the beginning of these blessings and with further experience we shall find a change for the better in our souls. These invisible things are precious to those who continue to meditate on them, and who delight to walk in the paths of faith and love.

Three final points follow on from what we have been considering:

1. We know that the wisdom, goodness, love, grace, mercy and power of God must be infinitely glorious as they exist in him. But they are only really understood by us when we have a satisfying and heart-warming

view of them as we see them working for the redemption of the church. Then their glory shines on us with refreshment and joy beyond description. As the apostle Paul exclaims: "Oh, the depth of the riches both of the wisdom and knowledge of God! . . . For of him and through him and to him are all things, to whom be glory for ever. Amen" (Romans 11:33—36).

2. It is through Christ that we believe in God (I Peter 1:21). So the final object of our faith is God himself; but we see his glory through Christ, who is the divinely appointed way of revealing God's glory.

3. Christ is the only way anyone can obtain a saving knowledge of God. The greatest religious thinkers of the world merely grope in the darkness of limited human understanding. As a flash of light on a dark night dazzles the eye instead of showing a traveller the way, so the light of the knowledge of God in Christ shines on the unbeliever in his darkness and yet he does not see the way because of unbelief. "Has not God made foolish the wisdom of this world? . . . But we preach Christ crucified, to the Jews a stumbling block and to the Greeks foolishness, but to those who are called, both Jews and Greeks, Christ the power of God and the wisdom of God" (I Corinthians 1:20—24).

Reference
1. This truth is explained in chapter three.

3.
The glory of Christ shown by the mystery of his two natures

The glory of Christ's two natures in one person is so great that the unbelieving world cannot see the light and beauty which shine from it. Many today deny the truth that Jesus Christ is both Son of God and Son of Man. But this is the glory which "angels desire to look into" (I Peter 1:12). Satan lifted himself up in pride against God in heaven and then tried to destroy human beings on earth who were made in the image of God. In his great wisdom, God united in his Son both these natures that Satan had sinned against. Christ, the God-man, triumphed over Satan through his death on the cross. Here is the foundation of the church. In creation, God "hangs the earth on nothing" (Job 26:7). But he founded his church on this immovable rock: "You are the Christ, the Son of the living God" (Matthew 16:16). This glorious fact is referred to in Isaiah 9:6: "For unto us a child is born, unto us a Son is given; and the government will be upon his shoulder. And his name will be called Wonderful Counsellor, Mighty God, Everlasting Father, Prince of Peace".

As the fire was in the bush Moses saw, so the fulness of the Godhead dwelt bodily in Christ, who was made flesh and dwelt among us (see Exodus 3:2; Colossians 2:9; John 1:14). The eternal fire of the divine nature dwelt in the bush of frail human nature; yet the human nature was not consumed. So we see "the favour of him

20

who dwelt in the bush" towards us sinners (Deuteronomy 33:16). As Moses was told to put off his shoes, so we should put away all imaginations and desires that come from our fallen human nature, that by the activity of our faith we may see the glory of Jesus Christ. I hope that what follows will stir us up to seek from God a spirit of wisdom and revelation to open the eyes of our understanding.

1. Let us be absolutely sure that this glory of Christ in his divine and human natures is the best, the most noble and the most useful object we can think about. The apostle Paul says that all other things are only loss and, in comparison, like dung (see Philippians 3:8—10). The scripture speaks of the foolishness of people in spending "money for what is not bread and wages for what does not satisfy" (Isaiah 55:2). They fix their thoughts on their sinful pleasures, refusing to take one look at the glory of Christ. Some rise to higher thoughts about the works of creation and providence, but there is no glory in these things compared with the glory of the two-fold nature of Christ. In Psalm 8 David is meditating on the greatness of the works of God. This makes him think of the poor, weak nature of man, which seems as nothing compared with those glories. But then he begins to admire the wisdom, goodness and love of God in exalting far above all the works of creation our human nature which was in Jesus Christ. The apostle explains this in Hebrews 2:5, 6.

How pleasant and desirable are the things of this world — wife, children, friends, possessions, power and honour! But the person who has all these things and also has a knowledge of the glory of Christ will say: "Whom have I in heaven but you? And there is none on earth that I desire besides you" (Psalm 73:25). For "who in the heavens can be compared to the

21

Lord? Who among the sons of the mighty can be likened to the Lord?" (Psalm 89:6). One glance at Christ's glorious beauty is enough to overcome and capture our hearts. If we are not frequently looking up to him to think about his glory, it is because our minds are too full of earthly things. Then we are not taking hold of the promise that our eyes shall see the King in his beauty.

2. One of the activities of faith consists in searching the scriptures, for they declare the truth about Christ (see John 5:39). We see the glory of Christ in the scriptures in three ways:

   i. By direct descriptions of his incarnation and his character as God-man. See Genesis 3:15; Psalm 2:7—9; 45:2—6; 78:17, 18; 110; Isaiah 6:1—4; 9:6; Zechariah 3:8; John 1:1—3; Philippians 2:6—8; Hebrews 1:1—3; 2:4—16; Revelation 1:17, 18.

   ii. By countless prophecies, promises and other expressions which all lead us to consider his glory.

   iii. By the patterns of divine worship God instituted in the Old Testament and by the direct testimony given to him from heaven in the New Testament. Isaiah says: "I saw the Lord sitting on a throne, high and lifted up, and the train of his robe filled the temple" (Isaiah 6:1). This vision of the divine Christ was so glorious that the seraphim (i.e. heavenly creatures in attendance) had to cover their faces. How much greater was the glory openly revealed in the days of the gospels! Peter tells us that he and other apostles were eye-witnesses of the majesty of the Lord Jesus Christ. "For he received from God the Father honour and glory when such a voice came to him from the Excellent Glory: This is my beloved Son, in whom I am well pleased" (II Peter 1:16, 17). We should be like the merchant seeking for all sorts of pearls. When he has found one of great price, he parts with all that he has to make it his own (see Matthew 13:45, 46). Every sacred truth in the scripture is a pearl which enriches us spiritually, but when we meet with the glory of Christ we shall find such joy that we shall never part with this pearl of great price. The glory of the Bible is that it is now the only tangible means of teaching us of the glory of Christ.

3. We must frequently meditate on the knowledge of the glory of Christ that we gain from the Bible. Our minds must be spiritual and holy, freed from earthly cares and affections. The person who never meditates with delight on the glory of Christ in the scriptures now will not have any real desire to see that glory in heaven. What sort of faith and love do people have who find time to think about many other things but make no time for meditating on this glorious subject?

4. Our thoughts should turn to Christ whenever there is opportunity at any time of the day. If we are true believers and if God's word is in our thoughts, Christ is near to us (see Romans 10:8). We shall find him ready to speak with us and hold communion with us. He says: "I stand at the door and knock" (Revelation 3:20). It is true there are times when he withdraws from us and we cannot hear his voice. But when this is so we must not be content. We should be like the bride in the Song of Solomon 3:1—4: "By night on my bed I sought the one I love; I sought him, but I did not find him. 'I will rise now', I said, 'And go about the city; in the streets, and in the squares I will seek the one I love.' I sought him, but I did not find him. The watchmen who go about the city found me, to whom I said, 'Have you seen the one I love?' Scarcely had I passed by them, when I found the one I love. I held him and would not let him go".

The experience of spiritual life in a Christian is

strong in proportion to his thoughts of, and delight in, the Christ who lives in him (see Galatians 2:20). If Christ has at any time been long out of our minds, we should rebuke ourselves.

5. All our thoughts about Christ and his glory should be accompanied by admiration, adoration and thanksgiving. We are commanded to love the Lord with all our souls, minds, and strength (see Mark 12:30). If we are true believers the grace of God works in our spiritually renewed minds and souls to help us do this. At the coming of Christ as Judge in the last day, believers will be filled with an overpowering sense of admiration at his glorious appearance, "when he comes, in that day, to be glorified in his saints and to be admired among all those who believe" (II Thessalonians 1:10). This admiration will develop into adoration and thanksgiving, an example of which is given in Revelation 5:9—13, where the whole church of the redeemed sings a new song. "And they sang a new song, saying, "You are worthy to take the scroll, and to open its seals; for you were slain, and have redeemed us to God by your blood out of every tribe and tongue and people and nation, and have made us kings and priests to our God; and we shall reign on the earth". Then I looked, and I heard the voice of many angels around the throne, the living creatures, and the elders; and the number of them was ten thousand times ten thousand, and thousands of thousands, saying with a loud voice: "Worthy is the Lamb who was slain to receive power and riches and wisdom, and strength and honour and glory and blessing!" And every creature which is in heaven and on the earth and under the earth and such as are in the sea, and all that are in them, I heard saying: "Blessing and honour and glory and power be to him who sits on the throne, and to the Lamb, for ever and ever!".

There are some people who hope to be saved by

Christ and to see his glory in another world but they are not concerned to meditate by faith on that glory in this world. They are like Martha who was worried about many things and not like Mary who chose the better part, sitting at the feet of Christ (see Luke 10:38—42). Let such be very careful lest they are not merely neglecting what they ought to do, but are actually despising it.

Some say they have a desire to behold the glory of Christ by faith, but when they begin to view this glory they find it too high and difficult. They are overcome, like the disciples on the Mount of Transfiguration. I admit that the weakness of our minds and our inability to understand much of the eternal glory of Christ prevents us from keeping our thoughts in a steady and unbroken meditation for any length of time. Those who are not practised in the skill of holy meditation in general will not be able to meditate on this mystery in particular. But even so, when faith can no longer hold open the eyes of our understanding to think about the Sun of righteousness shining in his beauty, at least we can still, by faith, rest in holy admiration and love.

4.
The glory of Christ as mediator:
(i) His humility

Adam's sin had put such a distance between mankind
and God that the whole human race would have been
completely ruined unless a suitable person could be
found to make peace between God and us, that is,
to act as a mediator. God could not act in this way and
there was no-one on earth who could do so. "Nor is
there any mediator between us, who may lay his hand
on us both" (Job 9:33). Yet a righteous peace between
God and man must be made by a mediator, or there
would never be any peace. Then the Lord Christ, as
the Son of God, said: "Sacrifice and offering you did
not desire, but a body you have prepared for me . . .
Behold, I have come . . . to do your will, O God."
(Hebrews 10:5—7). As the apostle Paul tells us, "there
is one God and one mediator between God and men,
the man Christ Jesus" (I Timothy 2:5). Christ emptied
himself and humbled himself when he "made himself
of no reputation . . . coming in the likeness of men"
(Philippians 2:7). This makes him glorious in the eyes
of believers, who are to seek this same kind of humility
for themselves. Let us look at three things:

1. The greatness of this humiliation. "God . . . dwells
on high (and) humbles himself to behold the things
that are in the heavens and in the earth" (Psalm 113:
5, 6). "All nations before him are as nothing and they
are counted by him less than nothing, and worthless"

(Isaiah 40:17). There is an infinite distance between God and his creatures, and it is an act of sheer grace for him to take notice of earthly things. Christ, as God, is completely self-sufficient in his own eternal blessedness. How great, then, is the glory of his self-humiliation in taking our nature that he might bring us to God! Such humiliation was not forced on him; he freely chose to do it.

2. The special nature of this humiliation. The Son of God did not cease to be equal with God when he became man. "Who, being in the form of God, did not consider it robbery to be equal with God" (Philippians 2:6). The Jews wanted to kill him because he said that "God was his Father, making himself equal with God" (John 5:18). When he took on him the form of a servant in our nature, he became what he had never been before, but he did not cease to be what he always had been in his divine nature. He who is God cannot ever cease to be God. The glory of his divine nature was veiled so that those who saw him did not believe he was God. Their reason could not understand something which had never been known before, that one and the same person should be both God and man. Yet those who believe know that he who is God humbled himself to take our nature for the salvation of the church, to the eternal glory of God. It is true that our Lord Jesus Christ is a stumbling-stone and a rock of offence to many today who, like Muslims and Jews, think of him only as a prophet. But take away the fact that he is God as well as man and all the glory, truth and power of Christianity is taken away with it.

There are three ways in which we can think of the true nature of the divine humiliation:

    i. Christ, the eternal Son of God, by an inexpressible act of his divine power and love, took on him our human nature and made it his own, just as his divine nature was his own. Human nature is common to us all but becomes special to us each individually when we are born, so that we are individuals different from everyone else. So the Lord Christ took that nature which is common to us all but made it especially his own, and became "the man, Christ Jesus".

ii. Because he was found on earth, living and suffering in our nature, the glory of his divine person was veiled. "He made himself of no reputation".

iii. Although he took our nature to be his own, he did not change it into something divine and spiritual but preserved it fully human. He really acted and suffered and was tried, tempted and forsaken, like any other man.

3. The glory of Christ in this humiliation. Even if we were angels, we could not describe the glory seen in the divine wisdom of the Father and the love of the Son in humbling himself to become a man. It is a mystery, because God is great and his ways are far above the understanding of his creatures. Yet it is the glory of the Christians' religion that he who was truly God made himself of no reputation, so that in comparison with others, he said he was "a worm, and no man" (Psalm 22:6). Are we burdened with a sense of sin? Are we perplexed with temptations? One look at this glory of Christ will support and relieve us. "He shall be as a sanctuary" (Isaiah 8:14). He who so emptied and humbled himself on our behalf, and yet lost nothing of his power as the eternal God, will save us from all our distresses. If we see no glory in this, it is because there is no spiritual knowledge or faith in us. The glory of Christ as mediator is the place of rest where the weary may rest, "and this is the refreshing" (Isaiah 28:12).

I urge you, therefore, to meditate by faith on the unique two-fold nature of Christ, with steady and practical purpose. As Christians we are to practise self-denial and be ready to take up our cross. We cannot do this without a proper consideration of the self-denial of the Son of God (see Philippians 2:5—8). What are the things of this world, even our loved ones and our own lives, which must soon come to an end, compared with the glory of Christ when he came to make himself of no reputation on this earth? When we begin thinking of these things, we soon come to a point where our human reasoning is left behind. I would like to be brought to this point every day. When we find the object on which our faith is fixed is too great and glorious for our understanding, we shall be filled with holy admiration, humble adoration, and joyful thanksgiving.

5.
The glory of Christ as mediator:
(ii) His love

There are many scriptures referring to the love of
Christ. For example, "the Son of God, who loved me
and gave himself for me" (Galatians 2:20); "By this
we know love, because he laid down his life for us"
(I John 3:16); "To him who loved us and washed us
from our sins in his own blood" (Revelation 1:5).
The brightest part of the glory of God is his love.
There is no terror in it but it is very attractive and
refreshing.

Christ became a mediator in the first place because
of the love of the Father, who chose to save a countless number of people through the shed blood of Christ.
And they are sanctified by the Spirit (see II Thessalonians 2:13; Ephesians 1:4–9). Because God is love,
any communication he makes with people must be in
love (I John 4:8, 9, 16). There was certainly nothing
in them to make God love them. Any good in anyone
is the effect of this great love of God (see Ephesians
1:4). God's love is the eternal source from which the
church receives its life through Christ.

Let us now consider the love of the Son, which is
full of compassion. Although sinful creatures, we
were capable of being recovered. God chose us as a
way to express his divine goodness and love. Christ
took our flesh and blood, not the nature of angels (see
Hebrews 2:14–16). He looked forward with great
delight to the salvation of mankind which would bring
such glory to God.

His willingness and delight in taking human nature were not lessened by the knowledge of the great difficulties he would have to face. In order to save us, he would have to continue until his soul was sorrowful to death. But this did not deter him. His love and mercy rose like the waters of a mighty stream, for he says: "Behold, I come; I delight to do your will, O my God" (Psalm 40:7, 8). So a body was prepared for him, to give effect to the immeasurable grace and fervent love he had for mankind. Now when we think of the glorious love of Christ, we find there is in his divine nature the love of God the Father. But there is more, because when he exercised his love he was human also. The love in the two natures is quite distinct and yet comes from the one person, Christ Jesus. It was an act of inexpressible love when he took our human nature, but it was an act of his divine nature only. His death was only an act of his human nature. But both were truly his acts, as we read in I John 3:16: "By this we know love, because he laid down his life for us".

I would urge you to prepare your minds continually for heavenly things by meditating seriously on the glory of the love of Christ. This cannot be done if the mind is always full of earthly thoughts. Do not be satisfied with general thoughts of the love of Christ but think of it in a more detailed way.

1. Consider whose love it is: the love of the Son of God who is also the Son of Man. As he is unique, so his love must be unique.

2. Think of the wisdom, goodness and grace shown in the eternal acts of his divine nature and of the pity and love of his human nature in all that he did and suffered for us (see Ephesians 3:19; Hebrews 2:14, 15; Revelation 1:5).

3. We deserved hatred, but, "in this is love, not that

we loved God, but that he loved us and sent his Son to be the propitiation for our sins" (I John 4:10). Christ's love is not lessened because we are spiritually unlovely.

4. What power this love has in its effect on our lives, enabling us to bear fruit to his glory.

So we may meditate on the teachings of scripture which contain the sweetness of the love of Christ. Do not be content only to have a right idea of the love of Christ in your minds but taste in your hearts that the Lord is gracious (see Song of Solomon 2:2–5). Christ is the food of our souls. There is no higher spiritual nourishment than his love to us which we should always desire.

6.
The glory of Christ as mediator:
(iii) His obedience

There was an unseen glory in all that Christ did and
suffered on earth. If people had seen it, they would
not have crucified the Lord of glory. Yet that glory
was revealed to some; the disciples "beheld his glory,
the glory as of the only begotten of the Father" (John
1:14).

Let us first look at the obedience of Christ in what
he did. He freely chose to obey. He said: "Behold,
I come to do your will, O God", before there was
any necessity for him to do that will. He was not
like us who, as human creatures, have always necessarily
been subject to the law of God. John the Baptist knew
that Jesus had no need to be baptised. But Christ
said: "Permit it to be so now, for thus it is fitting
for us to fulfil all righteousness" (Matthew 3:15).
Christ willingly identified himself with sinners when
he was baptised.

God gave him honour and glory, for by his obedience
the whole church was made righteous (see Romans
5:19). Christ's obedience to every part of the law
was perfect. The law was glorious when the ten
commandments were written by the finger of God.
It appears even more glorious when it is obeyed in
the hearts of believers. But it is only in the absolute
and perfect obedience of Christ that the holiness of
God in the law is seen in its full glory. "Though he
was a Son, yet he learned obedience by the things

which he suffered" (Hebrews 5:8). The Lord of all, who made all, lived in strict obedience to the whole law of God. Because he was such a unique person, his obedience possesses the glory of his uniqueness.

Now consider the glory of Christ's obedience as shown by what he suffered. No-one has ever been able to fathom the depths of the sufferings of Christ. We might look at him under the weight of the wrath of God, in his agony and sweat of blood, in his strong cries and tears. We might look at him praying, bleeding, dying, making his soul an offering for sin. "He was cut off from the land of the living; for the transgressions of my people he was stricken" (Isaiah 53:8). "Oh, the depth of the riches both of the wisdom and knowledge of God! How unsearchable are his judgments and his ways past finding out!" (Romans 11:33). How glorious is the Lord Christ in the eyes of redeemed believers!

Because Adam sinned, he and all his descendants stand before God ready to perish for ever under God's displeasure. In this state the Lord Christ comes to convinced sinners with his invitation: "Poor creatures! How sad is your condition! What has become of the beauty and glory of the image of God in which you were created? You are now in the deformed image of Satan and even worse, eternal misery lies before you. Yet look up once more; behold me! I will put myself in your place. I will bear that burden of guilt and punishment which would sink you to hell for ever. I will be made temporarily a curse for you, that you may have eternal blessedness".

Let us look at the glory displayed in the gospel: Jesus Christ is crucified before our eyes (see Galatians 3:1). We understand the scriptures only so far as we see in them the suffering and glory of Christ. The wisdom of the world sees nothing there but foolishness. "But even if our gospel is veiled, it is veiled to those who are perishing, whose minds the god of this world has blinded, who do not believe, lest the light of the gospel of the glory of Christ, who is the image of God, should shine on them" (II Corinthians 4:3, 4).

7.
The glory of Christ as mediator:
(iv) His exalted position

We shall now look at the glory of Christ which followed his sufferings. This is the same glory which he had with the Father before the foundation of the world. He prayed that his disciples might be with him where he was, to see his glory (see John 17:5, 24). While he was in the world in the form of a servant, this glory was veiled. When there is an eclipse of the sun, its beauty, light and glory are not seen for a time, so the full beauty, light and glory of Christ were temporarily eclipsed while he was on earth. His glory, however, will be seen with overwhelming joy and wonder by those who will be with him in heaven.

We know, too, that the same human nature which Christ had in this world is exalted now in glory. We cannot fully understand this but it is a basic belief of the true Christian. We do not know what we shall be like then; much less can we imagine what he will be like. This human nature of Christ Jesus does not merge into his divine nature in heaven. But it is filled with all the grace and perfection of which a created nature is capable. Believers will share this glory of the human nature of Christ. "We shall be like him, for we shall see him as he is" (I John 3:2). However, we shall never be like him to the same degree, for his glory is far above that of angels or men. "There is one glory of the sun, another glory of the moon, and another glory of the stars" (I Corinthians 15:41).

God the Father gave the greatest glory and dignity to Christ that can be given to any creature when he made him sit at the right hand of the majesty on high. God did this because of his infinite love to Christ and his delight in what he had done as mediator between God and mankind. Added to this is Christ's own unique glory in his divine wisdom, love and grace, fully displayed in the redemption of the church.

The glory which the Lord Jesus Christ actually possesses in heaven can only be understood by faith. Foolish people, using only their human imagination, have tried to represent this glory in pictures, but they do not know the scripture nor the eternal glory of the Son of God. We are not to imagine the image of a glorious person in heaven but to use our faith to meditate on the description of the glory of Christ given in the scripture. Let us not make the excuse that there will be time enough to consider these things when we get to heaven. If we do not have some knowledge by faith of the glory of Christ here and now, it means that we have no real desire for his presence in heaven.

We are all very selfish and are contented enough if our sins are forgiven and we are saved by Christ. But our faith and love should stir us up to put Christ and his concerns above everything else. Who is now surrounded with glory and power at the right hand of the majesty on high? It is he who was poor, despised, persecuted and killed for our sakes. It is the same Jesus who loved us and gave himself for us and redeemed us by his own blood. If we rightly value his love and share in any benefits arising from what he has done and suffered for his church, we can only rejoice in his present state and glory.

Blessed Jesus! We can add nothing to you, nor to your glory. But it is a joy to our hearts that you are so gloriously exalted at the right hand of God and we long to see that glory more fully and clearly, as you prayed, and promised, we should.

37

8.
The glory of Christ illustrated in the Old Testament

We know that the Old Testament is about the Lord Jesus Christ. Let us consider some of the ways in which the glory of Christ was foretold. First, a beautiful order of worship was given by God to Moses and through him to the people of Israel. There was the tabernacle (and later the temple) with the holy place, the ark, the mercy seat, the high priest, the sacrifices and the sprinkling of blood. But these were a mere shadow, looking forward to Christ as the one sacrifice for sin and his continuing activity as our great high priest. The Spirit of Christ was also in the prophets who spoke "beforehand of the sufferings of Christ and the glories that would follow" (I Peter 1:11).

As well as that outward worship pointing to the glory of Christ, there is Christ's inward communion with his church in love and grace illustrated in the Song of Solomon. This book is greatly neglected and misunderstood. A few days, or even a few hours, spent in the enjoyment of the loving communion with Christ so delightfully described in its pages would be a blessing far greater than all the treasures of the earth. If we, favoured as we are with the completed New Testament revelation of Christ, understand his glory less than Old Testament believers, we shall be judged unworthy to have received that New Testament!

Before Christ was born in Bethlehem, he sometimes appeared in the shape of a man. The Old Testament refers to him as being angry, or well-pleased, speaking as a man, and so points forward to the time when he would really become the man Jesus Christ.

When the law was given on Mount Sinai, it was full of the terror of death because no-one could meet its holy demands (see Exodus 19). But when Christ came to earth and fulfilled the law, he thereby procured pardon and righteousness for his people. Isaiah saw God's glory and was filled with terror until his sin was taken away by means of a coal from the altar. That was an illustration of the purifying power of Christ's sacrifice (see Isaiah 6:5–7; John 12:41). Isaiah also prophesies of the glory of Christ in coming into the world as a child. "Unto us a child is born, unto us a Son is given; and the government will be upon his shoulder. And his name will be called Wonderful Counsellor, Mighty God, Everlasting Father, Prince of Peace. Of the increase of his government and peace there will be no end". Though the prophets foretold the glory of the Christ who was coming, they did not fully understand what they said. But now, when every word of this revelation is made clear to us in the gospel, nothing but devilish pride in human hearts can blind them to the truth of Christ's glory seen in the Old Testament.

The promises and prophecies about the person of Christ, his coming, his kingdom and his glory, are like a line of life running through all the Old Testament. Christ explained these things and the wisdom, grace and love of God to the church in him, to his disciples, from the writings of Moses and all the prophets (see Luke 24:27, 44–46). We shall not benefit from reading the Old Testament unless we look for and meditate on the glory of Christ in its pages.

Lastly, God graciously helps us in our understanding by giving many names to the Lord Christ in the

Old Testament which show his excellence in different ways. Among others, he is called the rose and the lily, for the sweetness of his love and the beauty of his grace and obedience. He is called a pearl for his worth, a vine for his fruitfulness, a lion for his power and a lamb for his fitness for sacrifice. I mention these things not with any idea of studying them in detail here but simply to stimulate thought about such expressions and their meanings as they reveal something of the glorious character of Christ.

9.
The glory of Christ in his union with the church

Our union with Christ is so real that in the sight of God it is as though we had done and suffered what Christ did and suffered to redeem the church. He acted gloriously when he "bore our sins in his own body on the tree" and, "suffered once for sins, the just for the unjust, that he might bring us to God" (I Peter 2:24; 3:18). The purpose of our holy and righteous God was to save his church, but their sin could not go unpunished. It was, therefore, necessary that the punishment for that sin be transferred from those who deserved it but could not bear it, to one who did not deserve it but was able to bear it. This is the foundation of the Christian faith and all divine revelation contained in the scripture. Let us look a little further at this truth and consider how full it is of the glory of Christ.

1. It is not contrary to divine justice that some suffer punishment for the sins of others. I shall confirm this statement at this time only by saying that God, who can do no wrong, has often done so. When David sinned, seventy thousand men were destroyed by an angel, so that David said to the Lord: "I have sinned, and I have done wickedly; but these sheep, what have they done?" (II Samuel 24:15—17). When the children of Judah were taken captive, God punished them for the sins of their forefathers, especially those sins

41

committed in the days of Manasseh (see II Kings 23:26, 27). In finally destroying the Jewish nation, God punished them for shedding the blood of all the prophets from the beginning of the world (see Luke 11:50, 51).

2. There is always a special connection between those who sin and those who are punished. For instance, there is a relationship between parents and their children, or between a king and his subjects. There is also a sense of sharing in the punishment. The children of Israel were told: "Your sons shall be shepherds (wander) in the wilderness forty years, and bear the brunt of your infidelity" (Numbers 14:33). The punishment due to their sins was partly transferred to their children but part of their own punishment was also the knowledge of what would happen to the children.

3. There is a greater union and a closer relationship between Christ and the church than exists anywhere else in the world. This is seen in three ways:

i. There is a natural link between Christ and his church. God has made all people of one blood (see Acts 17:26). Every man is every other man's brother and neighbour (see Luke 10:36). This same relationship exists between Christ and the church. "As the children have partaken of flesh and blood, he himself likewise shared in the same. Both he who sanctifies and those who are being sanctified are all of one" (Hebrews 2:11, 14). In two aspects, however, there is a difference between the union of Christ with the church and the common brotherhood of mankind. He took our nature on him by a voluntary act of his own will but we had no choice in being related to one another by birth. Also he came into this union for only one purpose, that in our nature he might redeem the church: "that through death he might destroy him who had the power of death, that is, the devil, and release those who through fear of death were all their lifetime subject to bondage" (Hebrews 2:14, 15).

ii. There is a moral and spiritual union between Christ and the church. This is like the relationship between the head and the members of the body, or between the vine tree and its branches (see Ephesians 1:22, 23; John 15:1, 2). It is also like the bond between husband and wife. "Husbands, love your wives, just as Christ also loved the church and gave himself for it" (Ephesians 5:25). As he was head and husband of the church (which could only be saved and made holy by his blood and sufferings), it was fitting that he should so suffer, and it was right that the benefits of his sufferings should go to those for whom he suffered.

An objection may be raised that as it was "while we were still sinners, Christ died for us", there was no union between him and the church at that time (Romans 5:8). We are, it is said, joined to Christ by faith. Therefore, before our regeneration we were not joined to him. How then could he justly suffer on our behalf? I answer that it was the purpose of God, before Christ's sufferings, that the church of the elect should be his wife, so that he might love her and suffer for her. Jacob loved Rachel before she became his wife. He "served for a spouse and for a wife he tended sheep" (Hosea 12:12). Rachel is called Jacob's wife because of his love to her and because she was destined to be his bride before he was married to her. So God the Father gave all the elect to Christ, entrusting them to him, to be saved and sanctified. Christ himself says to the Father: "I have manifested your name to the men whom you have given me out of the world.

They were yours, and you gave them to me. I pray for them . . . whom you have given me, for they are yours" (John 17:6, 9).

iii. The third way in which Christ is united to his church is by the new covenant of which he is the pledge or surety. "Jesus has become a surety of a better covenant" (Hebrews 7:22). Here is the heart of the mystery of God's wise way of saving the church. The transfer of sins from sinners to Christ, who is in every way innocent, pure and righteous in himself is the life and soul of all scripture teaching. What Christ has done for us makes him glorious to us!

Let us consider the justice of God in forgiving sins. All of God's elect are sinners. How can God be just, then, if he allows them to go unpunished, seeing he did not spare the angels who sinned, nor Adam when he sinned at the first? The answer is in the union between Christ and the church. Because Christ represents the church in God's sight, God justly punishes him for all their sins so they are all freely and graciously pardoned (see Romans 3:24–26). At the cross, God's holiness and justice meet with his grace and mercy. This is the glory which delights the hearts and satisfies the souls of all who believe. How wonderful for them to see God rejoicing in his justice and yet at the same time showing mercy by giving them everlasting salvation! In the enjoyment of this glorious truth let me live, and in this faith let me die.

Christ is glorious, too, in his obedience to the law which he perfectly fulfilled. It was absolutely necessary that the law should be fulfilled but this could never be done by us. Through the union of Christ with the church, however, the law was fulfilled for us. "For what the law could not do, in that it was weak through the flesh, God did by sending his own Son in the likeness of sinful flesh, on account of sin: He condemned sin in the flesh, that the righteous requirement of the law might be fulfilled in us who do not walk according to the flesh but according to the Spirit" (Romans 8:3, 4).

An understanding by faith of this glory of Christ will scatter all the fears and remove all the doubts of poor tempted souls. Such knowledge will be an anchor to hold them firm in all the storms and trials of life, and in death.

10.
The glory of Christ shown in his giving himself to believers

The apostle Paul describes Christ giving himself to the church and the union between them as a great mystery (see Ephesians 5:32). Yet, though it is a mystery, we can still think about this relationship in which each believer can say: "My beloved is mine and I am his" (Song of Solomon 2:16). We must understand that Christ does not give himself to us because he is compelled to by some force. Nor does he come to us as an unreal dream. Nor does he become ours as we eat him in holy communion. He gives himself to believers in a special way, which I shall explain. Let us compare how God gave himself to mankind in the old creation, and then how Christ gives himself to the church in the new creation.

1. All life, power, goodness and wisdom were originally in God to an infinite degree. These and other perfections of his nature made up his essential glory.
2. In the old creation God communicated the glory of his goodness, power and wisdom (see Psalm 19:1; Romans 1:20) in a remarkable way, by causing one thing to be dependent on another. "I will answer, says the Lord, I will answer the heavens and they shall answer the earth. The earth shall answer with grain, with new wine, and with oil; and they shall answer Jezreel" (Hosea 2:21, 22). Living creatures depend on the earth; the earth depends on the sun and rain; there is a pattern of many things in harmony.

46

3. At the same time everything is dependent on God for the continual communication of his goodness and power to them all (see Acts 14:15—17; 17:24—29).

4. Mankind can by human reason see the glory of God in this work of creation and may learn his eternal power and Godhead. God's communication of himself in the creation is visible.

5. The glory of God seen in the creation is the glory of a Triune God. By his power and goodness the Father as the fountain of the Trinity framed the world; the Son carried out the plan of creation; and the Spirit of God continues to preserve all kinds of life on the earth (see John 1:1—3; Colossians 1:16; Hebrews 1:2; Genesis 1:2). "You hide your face, they are troubled; you take away their breath, they die and return to their dust. You send forth your Spirit, they are created; and you renew the face of the earth" (Psalm 104:29, 30).

Unless God had shown his glory visibly in the natural creation, no one but God himself could have known that he had such glory. Now we shall look at the new creation, the church, which is of a higher order than the material creation though the outward evidences of God's glory may not be so clearly seen there.

1. The goodness, grace, life, light, mercy and power which are the origins of the new creation are all in God. The whole purpose of the new creation, the church, is to show the glory of God by the ways he makes himself known to them, and through them to others.

2. In the first place it pleased God that the fulness of God's nature should be in Christ as head of the church (see Colossians 1:17—19). The goodness, grace, life, light, power and mercy which were necessary to create and preserve the church were to be in Christ and then communicated from him to the church.

3. Even though human nature was taken into personal union with the Son of God, all the fulness of God still lived in him (Colossians 2:9). He also received the Holy Spirit in all fulness and all the treasures of wisdom and knowledge were hidden in him (Colossians 2:3). These riches were in him, making him an excellent priest, prophet and king to his church.

4. In the creation of the world God first created the matter from which the earth was made, and then by the power of the Holy Spirit gave different forms of life to the different parts of the whole creation. So in the work of the new creation, even before the beginning of this world, God chose to set apart for himself that part of mankind which would make up his church. Then the work of the Holy Spirit was to make individual believers and form them into the glorious body of the church of Christ. What was said of the natural body is true of the body of Christ, the church. "My frame was not hidden from you, when I was made in secret, and skilfully wrought in the lowest parts of the earth. Your eyes saw my substance, being yet unformed. And in your book they all were written, the days were fashioned for me, when as yet there were none of them" (Psalm 139:15, 16). The substance of the church was under the eye of God when he chose its members. But they were not then individually formed, nor made into the body, although they were all written in God's book of life. In due course the Holy Spirit shaped them to the design of the body as purposed by God from the beginning.

5. The glorious existence of God as Trinity is shown in the divine order in which life is given to the church. The eternal source of all wisdom, grace, goodness and love is the Father. These divine qualities were in Jesus Christ, God's Son, who makes them available for the church. The Holy Spirit formed and gave spiritual life to each elect member of the church in every age, at his own time and season, to the glory of God.

In the same way, the whole new creation, the church, is preserved every day. Every moment there is vital power and strength, mercy and grace communicated from God the Father, Son and Holy Spirit to all believers in the world. This invisible communication is beyond the understanding of unbelieving people and for the most part they do not see the glory of it. Let us, however, join in the prayer of the apostle in Ephesians 1:17—23: "that the God of our Lord Jesus Christ, the Father of glory, may give to you the spirit of wisdom and revelation in the knowledge of him, the eyes of your understanding being enlightened; that you may know what is the hope of his calling, and what are the riches of the glory of his inheritance in the saints, and what is the exceeding greatness of his power towards us who believe, according to the working of his mighty power which he worked in Christ when he raised him from the dead and seated him at his right hand in the heavenly places, far above all principality and power and might and dominion, and every name that is named, not only in this age but also in that which is to come. And he put all things under his feet, and gave him to be head over all things to the church, which is his body, the fullness of him who fills all in all."

I shall now consider in more detail the way in which the Lord Christ communicates himself and the blessings he has to give to all those who believe. We receive him by faith. "As many as received him, to them he gave the right to become children of God, even to those that believe in his name" (John 1:12). In order that we may receive him, he must be given. The Father gave Christ freely to us. This was his eternal purpose. He also gave all the elect to Christ, as he said: "They were yours, you gave them to me" (John 17:6). He promised Christ in the gospel to all believers and by his almighty power created faith in the souls of the elect, enabling them to receive Christ (see Ephesians 1:19, 20; 2:5—8).

But we are thinking mainly of the way in which Christ himself comes down to our level and shows us the glory of his wisdom and love.

1. He gave to us his Holy Spirit (see Romans 8:9; I Corinthians 6:17). When Christ came into the world he took our nature into union with his own. When we are born again he takes us into a spiritual union with himself. He becomes ours and we are his. This is something inexpressibly glorious. There is nothing like it in the whole creation. The same Spirit is in Christ the head and in his church, giving life and directing the whole body. See the glory, the honour and security of the church! The privilege of understanding how the nature of the church displays the glory of God is to be preferred above all the wisdom of the ungodly world.

2. So we have a new nature which is Christ's own nature formed in us. We are made partakers of his divine nature in varying degrees through the precious promises of the gospel. This divine nature in believers is called the new man, the new creature, the spirit which is born of the Spirit, being changed into the image of Christ, and the workmanship of God (see John 3:6; Romans 6:3—8; II Corinthians 3:18; 5:17; Ephesians 4:20—24; II Peter 1:4). His giving to us of his nature is how Christ is made to us wisdom and sanctification. He says of his church: "This is now bone of my bone and flesh of my flesh. I see myself, my own nature, in them, and they are attractive and desirable to me". So eventually he will "present it to himself a glorious church, not having spot or wrinkle or any such thing, but that it should be holy and without blemish" (Ephesians 5:27).

3. Two effects follow from being in Christ by faith. The first is a continual supply of spiritual life, grace and strength. The members of his church live, yet not they but Christ lives in them, and the life which they live in the flesh is by the faith of the Son of God (see Galatians 2:20). The other effect is that Christ's righteousness is counted as our righteousness and we receive all the benefits which come from him, as our mediator (see Romans 4:5).

We could think of other ways in which the love of Christ is made known to us. It is, for example, shed abroad in our hearts by the Holy Ghost, and our love returns to him by the almighty power of the same Spirit (Romans 5:5). I hope, however, that we have thought enough about the glory of the way Christ gives himself to the church for our hearts to be filled with holy wonder and thanksgiving.

11.
The glory of Christ shown by his gathering together all things in himself

". . . which he made to abound toward us in all wisdom and prudence, having made known to us the mystery of his will, according to his good pleasure which he purposed in himself, that in the dispensation of the fullness of the times he might gather together in one all things in Christ, both which are in heaven and which are on earth -- in him" (Ephesians 1:8--10).

In trying to understand these words we must consider the original state of all things in heaven and earth, the disorder brought about by sin and the glory of their restoration by Christ.

1. God calls himself "I AM" (Exodus 3:14). He is eternally self-existent and the source of all existence. Everything that exists is from him (Romans 11:36). Similarly, God is the source of all goodness.
2. Where there is a being of such infinite goodness, there is also infinite blessedness and happiness, to which nothing can be added. The blessedness and self-satisfaction of God were just the same before he created anything as they are now. This blessedness consists in the mutual, eternal love of the three holy persons, Father, Son and Spirit, as one God. When God acts, he does so in the perfect knowledge and perfect love of his own perfections.
3. God made all things according to his own will and pleasure, acting in infinite wisdom, power and

goodness. What he gave to things outside himself was a limited, dependent existence and goodness. He said: "Let there be", and they were. "Then God saw everything that he had made, and indeed it was very good" (Genesis 1:31). Existence and goodness in creation must be the first outward way in which the divine nature shows to us God's glory. The continuance of all creation also depends on God.

4. So, "in the beginning God created the heavens and the earth" (Genesis 1:1). He appointed the earth for people to live in and prepared heaven as a dwelling place for the angels. According to their different natures, those locations also brought glory and praise to God. This order of things was very beautiful. There was no break in fellowship between God and those he had created. He communicated directly with them and all that they did was in obedience to him.

5. But this beautiful order was disturbed and broken by the entrance of sin. Part of the family of angels in heaven, and the whole family of mankind on earth, fell from their dependence on God and only hatred and confusion remained among them. Because the earth had been put in subjection to mankind, who had now fallen, God cursed the earth. He did not, however, curse the heavens because many of the angels remained unfallen. The angels who sinned were completely rejected for ever. Although the whole human race had fallen through sin, God determined to save part of it by his grace.

6. The plan of God was now to bring the two families, angels and mankind, together under a new head; the good angels having been preserved from sinning and all believing people being delivered from their sins. This is the meaning of the words: to "gather together in one all things in Christ, both which are in heaven and which are on earth — in him" (Ephesians 1:10); and to "reconcile all things to himself . . . whether things on

earth or things in heaven" (Colossians 1:20). Jesus Christ, the Son of God, is the new head in whom God has gathered together all things in heaven and earth into one. As one body and one family they are now dependent on him by whom they live and have their existence. God the Father has "put all things under (Christ's) feet, and gave him to be head over all things to the church, which is his body, the fullness of him who fills all in all. He is before all things, and in him all things consist. And he is the head of the body, the church, who is the beginning, the firstborn from the dead, that in all things he might have the pre-eminence. For it pleased the Father that in him all fullness should dwell" (Ephesians 1:22, 23; Colossians 1:17–19).

7. God has given all power in heaven and earth to the head of this new godly family. All must now come to Christ for spiritual power, grace and goodness. Whether angelic or human, both are now completely dependent on him. Unfallen angels had no need of redemption and grace and so were capable of continuing existence in the glory of heaven. But it was necessary for us that Christ should take our nature and unite himself to us by his Spirit. So believers are redeemed to live in a glorious heaven, one family with the angels.[1]

A few further thoughts may help us to meditate on the gathering together of all things in Jesus Christ, the glory of which is far beyond our understanding.

1. Christ alone could bear the weight of this glory. The Holy Spirit describes him as, "the brightness of (the Father's) glory and the express image of his person, and upholding all things by the word of his power" (Hebrews 1:3). "He is the image of the invisible God, the firstborn over all creation. For by him all things were created that are in heaven and that are on earth,

54

visible and invisible, whether thrones or dominions or principalities or powers. All things were created through him and for him. And he is before all things, and in him all things consist" (Colossians 1:15—17).

2. It was the wonderful, eternal purpose of God to glorify himself by Christ being made man. This purpose was that the whole creation, especially the church which was to be eternally blessed, should have a new head. The order of the whole family in heaven and earth, angels and people, was to be dependent on Christ. Nothing ought to fill believers' hearts with delight and joy more than this view by faith of the divine beauty in the gathering together of all things in Christ.

3. The sin which destroyed the beauty and order of creation has been dealt with. Everything that at the creation was beautiful, because of the way it was all dependent on God, displayed the beauty and wisdom of God. The entrance of sin ruined that scene of beauty. But now in the gathering together of all things in Christ Jesus, everything in Christ is restored again to fellowship with God. Indeed, the whole marvellous framework of the divine creation has been made more beautiful than it was before and this all arises from its new relation to the Son of God.

4. God is always wise in whatever he does. His infinite wisdom and power were seen in the first creation. "O Lord, how manifold are your works! In wisdom you have made them all" (Psalm 104:24). But when the effects of this divine wisdom were spoiled, greater wisdom was required to restore them. In bringing together again all things in Christ, God showed his unsearchable wisdom to the angels, who had not known before what his purposes were. "To the intent that now the manifold wisdom of God might be made known by the church to the principalities and powers in the heavenly places." (Ephesians 3:10). In him are

hid and by him are displayed all the treasures of wisdom (Colossians 2:3).

5. In the first creation, glorious as it was, everything depended directly on God and the law of obedience to him. This was a fragile unity, depending on the willingness of creatures to obey the creator. But everything in the new creation, including every believer, has been gathered together into Christ the head. This is an unbreakable unity. They who depend entirely on Christ for their eternal security cannot now fall away from the safety they enjoy in him.

Reference
1. Owen uses 13 arguments in this passage which have been summarised into 7 paragraphs.

12.
The difference between faith's present view of the glory of Christ and our seeing it in heaven

"We walk by faith, not by sight" (II Corinthians 5:7). In this life, faith; in the life to come, sight. They are the abilities of the soul which make it aware of the glory of Christ.

Faith's view of the glory of Christ in this world is dark and hazy. As the apostle says: "Now we see . . . dimly" (I Corinthians 13:12). Our knowledge is not direct, but is like an imperfect reflection of the reality. The gospel, without which we could not discover Christ at all, is still very far from fully displaying the greatness of his glory. This is because we ourselves imperfectly understand it. Our faith is weak and imperfect. There is no part of his glory we can fully understand. In our present earthly state there is something like a wall between us and Christ. But sometimes we see him through the windows. "Behold, he stands behind our wall; he is looking through windows, gazing through the lattice" (Song of Solomon 2:9). These windows are the opportunities we have of hearing and receiving the promises of the gospel in the means of grace and the ministry of the word. Such opportunities are full of refreshment to the souls of those who believe. But the view of his beauty and glory does not last. Then we cry: "As the deer pants for the water brooks, so pants my soul for you, O God. My soul thirsts for God, for the living God. When shall I come and appear before God?" (Psalm 42:1, 2). When shall I see him again, even if it is only through a window?

Sometimes, like Job, we cannot see him because he hides his face behind a cloud (see Job 23:8, 9). At other times he shows himself as the sun in all its strength and we cannot bear its brightness.

Now, by comparison, let us consider how we will see the same glory of Christ when we are in heaven. Our sight will be immediate, direct and steady.

1. Christ himself with all his glory will be really and continually with us. We shall no longer have to be satisfied with the mere descriptions of him that we have in the gospel. We shall see him face to face (I Corinthians 13:12) and as he is (I John 3:2). We shall see him with our bodily eyes, for Job says: "In my flesh shall I see God (my Redeemer), whom I shall see for myself, and my eyes shall behold" (Job 19: 25—27). Our bodily senses will be restored and glorified in a way we cannot now understand, in order that we may be able to look at Christ and his glory for ever and ever. We shall see not only his human nature but his divinity also in its infinite wisdom, love and power. That glory will be a thousand times more than anything we can imagine.

This sight of Christ is what all the saints of God long for. It is their desire "to depart and be with Christ, which is far better; to be absent from the body and to be present with the Lord" (Philippians 1:23; II Corinthians 5:8). Those who do not often have this longing are earthly and unspiritual people.

2. No-one in this life has the power, either spiritually or bodily, to see the glory of Christ as it really is. When some reflections of his divine glory were seen on the Mount of Transfiguration, the disciples were confused and very much afraid. If the Lord Jesus came to us now in his majesty and glory, we would be incapable of receiving any benefit or comfort from his appearance. The apostle John, whom he loved, fell at his feet as dead

when he appeared to him in his glory (Revelation 1:17). Paul and all those who were with him fell to the earth when the brightness of his glory shone on them as they journeyed to Damascus (see Acts 26:13, 14).

What an insult it is to God when foolish people try to make pictures and images of the Lord Christ in his present glory! The only way we can know him now is by faith, dimly. We cannot know him now as he truly is, full of indescribable glory.

Because of our sinful natures, our minds were completely dark and evil, being unable to see spiritual things in a proper light. We have been partly restored by grace and have become light in the Lord (Ephesians 5:8). But our minds are still imprisoned in our natural bodies and many weaknesses and imperfections remain. These will be gone for ever in heaven (see Ephesians 5:27). After the resurrection our minds and bodies will be free from everything that has prevented us from enjoying a full view of the glory of Christ. Then one pure act of spiritual sight in looking on the glory of Christ, one pure act of love in clinging to God, will make us far happier and more satisfied than we could ever be with all our religious activities.

We have a natural power to understand and judge things in this present earthly life. But this natural ability cannot help us to see and understand spiritual things, as the apostle shows us in I Corinthians 2:11, 14: "What man knows the things of a man except the spirit of the man which is in him? Even so, no one knows the things of God except the Spirit of God . . . The natural man does not receive the things of the Spirit of God, for they are foolishness to him; nor can he know them, because they are spiritually discerned".

So God gives us the supernatural ability of faith and grace. We still have our natural understanding but it is only by spiritual ability that we see spiritual things. In heaven there will be the added ability to see glory.

59

1. As spirituality does not destroy but improves natural ability, so the ability to comprehend glory will not destroy the powers of faith and grace, but will perfect them absolutely.

2. By nature we cannot clearly understand the essence of grace which is seen only by those who receive it. So by grace we cannot fully understand the nature of glory, which is seen perfectly only when we are changed and living in glory.

3. The best idea we can get of the nature of glory is to consider that the moment it shines on us we shall be changed into the perfect likeness of Christ.

There is a progression from nature to glory. Grace renews nature, glory makes grace perfect and so finally the whole soul is brought to its rest in God. The blind man saw men as trees walking when the Saviour first touched his eyes. At the Saviour's second touch, he saw everything clearly (see Mark 8:22—25). This is like the difference between the sight of grace and the sight of glory.

Having thought of our minds, now let us think of our glorified bodies. After we are risen from the grave, we shall see our Redeemer. Stephen actually saw, "the glory of God and Jesus standing at the right hand of God" (Acts 7:55). Who would not wish to have shared the privilege of the disciples who physically saw Christ while he was on earth? He told them that "many prophets and righteous men desired to see what you see" (Matthew 13:17). If this was such a great privilege, how glorious it will be when, with our eyes purified and strengthened, we shall see Christ in the fullness of his glory! We cannot imagine what it will be like but we know he prayed to his Father that we should be where he is, to see the greatness and beauty of his glory (see John 17:24).

While we are here in this world "we ourselves groan

within ourselves, eagerly waiting for the adoption, the redemption of our body" (Romans 8:23). Like Paul, we cry: "O wretched man that I am! who will deliver me from this body of death?" (Romans 7:24). The nearer anyone is to heaven, the more earnestly he desires to be there, because Christ is there. Our thoughts of Christ are so confused and imperfect that they usually end in our longing to be able to know him better. But this is the best state of mind we can be in here! I pray God I may never be delivered from it and that the Lord would increase such desires more and more in all who believe.

The heart of a believer, affected by the glory of Christ, is like a needle touched by a magnet. It can no longer be quiet or satisfied at a distance, although its movements are weak and trembling. It is continually pressing towards him but will not come to its rest in this world. But there in heaven, with Christ continually before us, we shall be able to look steadily at him in all his glory. This constant view will bring an ever-lasting refreshment and joy to our souls. We cannot understand, however, what the final vision of God will be like. But we know that the pure in heart shall see God (Matthew 5:8), and even in eternity Christ will be the only means of communication between God and the church.

Let us look for a moment at the Old Testament saints. They saw something of the glory of Christ but only in the form of veiled symbols. They longed for the time when the veil would be removed and the symbols give place to reality. They looked for the fulfilment of all the divine promises about the coming of the Son of God into the world. There was often more of the power of true faith and love in their hearts than is found among most believers today. When Jesus actually came, old Simeon took the child in his arms and said: "Now Lord let me depart, now let me die, this is what my soul has longed for" (see Luke 2:28, 29).

We have a clearer revelation of the unique nature of Christ and of his work than those saints of old. And the view we shall have of Christ's glory in heaven will be much clearer and far brighter even than the revelation we now have. If those old saints prayed so long for the removal of the veils and symbols and desired so earnestly to see the glory of Christ, how much more earnestly should we be praying to see his glory?

We have now thought of the glory of Christ as being shown in three degrees. The Old Testament saints under the law had the symbols. In the gospel we have the perfect likeness. But we must wait for heaven where Christ is, to enjoy the reality.

Let us examine ourselves to see whether we are pressing forward continually towards the perfect view of the glory of Christ in heaven. If we are not, it is a sure sign that our faith is not real. If Christ is in us, he is "the hope of glory" (Colossians 1:27). Many love the world too well to wish to get through it quickly to a place where they may see the glory of Christ. Their interest is in their possessions, their business, or family. Such people see the beauty of this world in the mirror of self-love and their minds are changed into the same selfish image! On the other hand, true believers, delighting to see the glory of Christ in the gospels, are changed into his image.

Our Lord Jesus Christ alone perfectly understands the eternal blessedness which will be enjoyed by those who believe in him. He prays that they may "be with me where I am, that they may behold my glory" (John 17:24). If we can at present understand only a little of what glory means, at least we ought to trust the wisdom and love of Christ that it will be infinitely better than anything we can enjoy here. Should we not be continually desiring to be included in his prayer?

62

13.
Another difference between faith's present view of the glory of Christ and our seeing it in heaven

When we look at something at a great distance, it disappears from our view if something comes in between. So it is sometimes with our faith. We have very little, or no sight at all, of the glory of Christ. While we are in this life, the Lord Christ in his sovereign wisdom sometimes hides himself from us. Job complained that he could not see God on the left hand or on the right (see Job 23:8, 9). Isaiah writes: "Truly you are God who hide yourself, O God of Israel, the Saviour" (Isaiah 45:15). The Psalmist cried: "How long, Lord? Will you hide yourself for ever?" (Psalm 89:46).

Sometimes when listening to the preaching of the word, the sight of Christ's glory is hidden from some, while at the same time others are warmed and strengthened (see John 14:22)! I must now try to answer two questions:

1. Why does the Lord Christ sometimes hide himself and his glory from the faith of believers? There are many reasons but I will mention only one. He does it to stir us up to search for him with all our heart. Our wretched laziness so often makes us neglect meditation on heavenly things. But Christ is patient with us. He knows that those who have seen something of his glory, although they have not valued it as they ought, cannot bear his absence for long. He says: "I will return again

to my place, till they acknowledge their offence. Then they will seek my face; in their affliction they will diligently seek me" (Hosea 5:15). Then we should be like the bride who sought her beloved but at first could not find him. She said: "I will rise now and will seek the one I love". And when she had found him, she "held him and would not let him go" (see Song of Solomon 3:1–5). So often we are like the man described by the prophet to Ahab the king: "While your servant was busy here and there, he was gone" (I Kings 20:40). Christ commits himself to us and we ought not to let him go. But while we are busy here and there, our minds become occupied too much with other things. He leaves us and we cannot find him.

2. How can we know when Christ takes his presence from us so that we cannot see his glory? I am speaking now only to those whose chief concern is to keep their faith and love active towards Jesus Christ. The effect of his presence is to make us try to live like him and greatly love him. But it is only while we are conscious of living by faith that we have this great desire to be like him. Growing like Christ means growth in grace, holiness and obedience. When this growth seems to stop we may know Christ is not with us.

There are those whose natural minds may be affected by looking at images and crucifixes. But the effect which is produced by an image is only a natural effect. An imaginary Christ will not have a spiritual effect on peoples' minds. It is only by the spiritual knowledge of the glory of Christ by faith that grace is given to make the soul willing to be gladly changed into his likeness. If our hearts grow cold and lifeless in spiritual duties, it is certain that the Lord Christ has left us for a while. It is just as certain that when we are really looking by faith on the glory of Christ in the gospel and continue in holy thought and meditation, we shall feel his life and grace working in us. Let us put this to the test and find how our love to him will grow. We shall then also love all who belong to him. It is by the activity of our faith in Christ that the Holy Spirit renews our souls by his transforming power.

We come to Christ in the first place that we may have life. But we also come to him as believers that we might have life more abundantly (John 10:10). As he reproaches those who would not come to him that they might have life, so he could justly reprove us all for not coming more often to him, by faith, in order that we might have this life more abundantly.

There are many who say they are Christians, who live a very careless life, without any concern for real spiritual blessings. They do not know the holy spiritual refreshment which the Lord Christ brings to us by his Spirit, the Comforter. Such blessings include spiritual peace, refreshing comforts, inexpressible joys and blessed assurance. Without some experience of these things, our Christianity is heartless, lifeless and useless. How can we say we believe the promises about the eternal glories of heaven if we do not believe the promise of the enjoyment of these spiritual blessings here and now?

Christ says to anyone who loves him: "I will love him and manifest myself to him . . . and my Father will love him, and we will come to him and make our home with him" (John 14:21, 23). When he comes and shows himself to us, he always brings with him peace, comfort, joy and assurance. We feast with him by means of these spiritual refreshments (see Revelation 3:20). If we ask how we receive such blessings, the answer is, by looking on the glory of Christ by faith (see I Peter 1:9, 10). Let us meditate on the glory of Christ's unique nature, his humbling of himself in coming to this world, his present position in the highest heaven, his love and his grace. Our hearts will then be affected in some degree by a sense of his love, which is the source of all our spiritual comforts (see John 4:14; Romans 5:5). When we lose these blessings, we know that the presence of Christ has left us for a while and we cannot see his glory.

Now the purpose of the Lord Christ in hiding his glory from our view is to stir us up to use the grace he has given us and to seek him with all our heart. Do we feel lifeless and joyless, without a sense of his love in our hearts? There is no way of recovery but to turn to Christ. All our spiritual troubles arise from ourselves, from the evil desires which remain in us, often increased by Satan's temptations. We must take a steady view of the glory of Christ by faith alone and this will bring back life, joy and love to our hearts and souls.

If we are satisfied with a mere idea of the glory of Christ as a piece of information obtained from scripture, we shall find it has no transforming power for our lives. Let us love Christ with full purpose of heart; let our minds be filled with thoughts of delight in him; let our trust in him be constantly exercised; then virtue will proceed from him to purify our hearts, increase our holiness, strengthen our graces and fill us sometimes with "joy inexpressible and full of glory" (I Peter 1:8). It is good if the love of our heart is quickened at the same time as our understanding is enlightened. Mere knowledge and no love leads to empty formality. All love and no knowledge leads to superstition.

In believers themselves, where there is a love of the world and of the things of this life, faith is weakened and the mind becomes unsteady in its view of the glory of Christ. But everyone who has a spiritual view of Christ's glory will have a great love for him and the mind will be filled with thoughts about him (see Philippians 3:8—10; Colossians 3:1, 2).

Wherever the gospel is preached, Satan blinds the minds of them who do not believe, "lest the light of the gospel of the glory of Christ, who is the image of God, should shine on them" (II Corinthians 4:4). But God overpowers him in the salvation of the elect and shines into their hearts "to give the light of the knowledge of the glory of God in the face of Jesus Christ" (II Corinthians 4:6). But Satan does not give up. He uses all sorts of ways to trouble the minds of believers. His fiery darts make fears and doubts arise so that they cannot feel the love of Christ. He makes others careless so that they do not examine themselves to see whether Christ is in them or not (see II Corinthians 13:5). In this way a great many give up seeking an experience of the power and grace of the gospel in their own souls and so they never discover the glories of Christ that they could know.

It is now time to consider the sight we shall have of the glory of Christ in heaven.

1. The ability and activity of our souls will be made perfect. We shall be as "the spirits of just men made perfect" (Hebrews 12:23). We shall be free from all the limitations of the flesh. We shall be changed to become perfect, in purity and holiness, like God. Our glorified bodies will be able to enjoy the glory of Christ for ever. Our understanding will be perfect as we see God, and all the affections of our heart will be inseparably fixed in him. In our present state of weakness we are forced sometimes to turn aside from considering these realities, just as we turn away our eyes from the brightness of the sun. But in that perfect state, we shall be able to look steadily at the glory with eternal delight. Says David: "As for me, I will see your face in righteousness; I shall be satisfied when I awake in your likeness" (Psalm 17:15). We shall never become tired of looking at Christ, who alone

is the likeness and image of God. Here we walk by faith but there we shall be given an eternal power of sight with which to see him as he is, face to face, with perfect enjoyment for evermore (see Revelation 4:8).

2. To be in hell under the wrath of God is in itself the greatest evil possible. But to be there for ever, without any end to its misery, must be an evil far beyond our power to imagine or describe. So with the eternal life of future blessedness, there will be no limitation of time, no interruption of enjoyment. We shall be "always . . . with the Lord" (I Thessalonians 4:17). There will be no need of any of our present means of worship. The constant, immediate, uninterrupted enjoyment of God and the Lamb will supply all that we need. "The Lord God Almighty and the Lamb are its temple. And the city had no need of the sun or of the moon to shine in it, for the glory of God illuminated it, and the Lamb is its light" (Revelation 21:22, 23). In heaven the perpetual presence of Christ with his saints makes it one continuous experience of light and glory. There will be no doubts or fears for we shall be in a perpetual state of triumph over them (see I Corinthians 15:55–57). The view of the glory of Christ will be always the same, yet always new, with nothing to disturb the mind in the most perfect enjoyment of a blessed life centred on the most perfect object, the glory of Christ. This experience is the greatest blessedness of which our human natures are capable.

14.
Further differences between faith's present view of the glory of Christ and our seeing it in heaven

1. At present we gain a spiritual understanding of the glory of Christ by faith as we study the scriptures. But the light of revelation is distributed through all the books of the Old and New Testaments, just as natural light is given to us through the sun, moon and stars. If all the light were channelled through one source, we could not bear it. So in the scriptures the glory of Christ is described little by little in various ways. Sometimes it is in plain words; at others in types and figures which illustrate his humility and love to us. Different truths are scattered in the Bible for us to collect as lovely flowers. In Song of Solomon 5:10–16 the bride considers the many beauties of her loved one and concludes that "he is altogether lovely". So we, slowly discovering the many beauties of Christ, find him to be altogether glorious.

In heaven, however, the whole glory of Christ will be before us. We shall be able, in the light of glory, to take it all in. Here we cannot imagine what beauty and glory there will be in this complete discovery of Christ. We shall understand all at once what he did and suffered, his present exalted position, his union with the church, and how all things are gathered together in him. We shall see the glory of God, his wisdom, righteousness, grace, love, goodness and power, all shining eternally in Christ. We can long for this here below and even now have a taste of it, but the whole knowledge of Christ is in his heavenly glory where there are the waters of life and rivers of pleasure for evermore.

2. The sight we shall have of the glory of Christ in heaven will change us perfectly and wholly into his likeness. "We shall be like him for we shall see him as he is" (I John 3:2). Let us notice this in a little more detail.

    i. When the soul leaves the body, it is immediately freed from all weakness, disability, darkness and fear. The sinful nature no longer exists. Death was God's judgment on sin, but through the death of Christ for us we receive mercy (see I Corinthians 15:54). Unbelievers, however, must receive the reward of their unbelief — the banishing of their souls from God.

    ii. Believers, having been freed from the burden of their sinful natures, find that their spirits can fulfil the purpose for which they were created. They can enjoy God with a delightful ease and satisfaction. Then, too, at the resurrection, the new glorified body will never hinder but help in all spiritual activities. Our eyes were made to see our Redeemer and all our other senses will be used to enjoy fellowship with him.

    iii. We shall not be brought into the immediate presence of Christ without a new power being given us, a heavenly ability, to see the Lord Christ as he is. This glorious ability will take the place of faith which we need only in this life.

    iv. When believers first see the glory of Christ, they will be at once completely changed into his likeness. When sin entered the world and Adam was driven out of the garden of Eden, God said, in condemning him, "Man is become as one of us, to know good and evil" (Genesis 3:22). When the work of grace is finished, God can say, in similar

words, not in anger, but in love and infinite goodness, "Man is become like one of us." In this life
our faith in Christ does bring about gradual change
in us, though incompletely. We must have some
experience now of such changes if we would be
sure of being perfectly restored eternally in the
likeness of God (see II Corinthians 3:18; 4:16—18;
Philippians 3:10—14).

3. Even in heaven, all creatures must eternally live in
dependence on God, the eternal fountain of life, goodness and blessedness. We shall be no more self-sufficient
in glory than we are now. Everything will come to us
through Christ Jesus, all things in heaven and earth
being gathered together in him (see Ephesians 1:10, 11).
Our continuing in a state of happiness and glory will
depend entirely on these communications from God
through Christ. So we shall never grow tired of seeing
Christ in heaven. The infinite object of our glorified
sight will be unfathomable and always new to our
finite understanding. Our happiness will consist in
continually fresh communications from the infinite
fullness of God's nature.

This future life of glory is so much greater than the
life of faith we now live. Yet there is no present earthly
joy or satisfaction that can compare with faith's weak
and imperfect view of the glory of Christ. Even faith's
poor view gives us such a taste of future blessedness in
the enjoyment of Christ that we are stirred up to sigh
and long for the time when we shall see him, be for
ever with him, and know him as he knows us.

15.
An urgent call to those who are not yet true believers in Christ

Often in the Gospels, whenever there is any description of the excellence of Christ as a Saviour, there is also an invitation to sinners to come to him. So we are right in these closing chapters of our study of the glory of Christ to relate this truth to our needs as sinners. Christ says: "Come to me, all you who labour and are heavy laden, and I will give you rest" (Matthew 11:28). And, "If anyone thirsts, let him come to me and drink" (John 7:37). There are several reasons why we should heed this invitation:

1. Many hear the word preached but few are saved. "Many are called but few are chosen" (Matthew 22:14). It is the greatest folly in the world to leave the consideration of our eternal state to some uncertain future time which may never come.
2. Do not think that because you profess to be a Christian and enjoy the outward blessings of the gospel, you necessarily belong to Christ. You may compare yourselves with others and think you are better than some. But if you rely for your salvation on anything that you are, or anything you do, you will eternally deceive your souls (Matthew 3:9).
3. Unless we are thoroughly convinced that without Christ we are under the eternal curse of God, as the worst of his enemies, we shall never flee to him for refuge. Christ did not come "to call the righteous,

but sinners, to repentance" (Matthew 9:13). So our chief concern, if we are not yet saved, should be to have a deep sense of the wretched and lost condition of our souls.

4. But now consider the infinite love of Christ in calling you to come to him for life, mercy, grace, peace and eternal salvation. There are so many encouragements given in scripture that are so suitable for lost, convinced sinners. Jesus Christ still stands before sinners calling, inviting, encouraging them to come to him. Through the preaching of Christian ministers, Christ says: "Why will you die? Why will you not have pity on your souls? Come to me and I will remove all your sins, sorrows, fears and burdens. I will give rest to your souls". Consider the greatness of his mercy, grace and love in so earnestly calling you to him. Do not let the poison of unbelief, which inevitably leads to eternal ruin, make you despise this holy invitation to come to Christ.

5. Perhaps you begin to come to him and are afraid he will not receive you because you have been too great a sinner. But the language of the gospel is that Christ is ready to receive every sinner who comes to him. The Father, the Son and the Holy Spirit all agree that the Lord Christ is ready to receive all sinners who come to him. Nothing but obstinate unbelief, which makes God a liar, can suggest that he is not willing to receive us when we come to him.

6. Consider that Christ is as able to save us as he is ready to receive us. He will not save unbelieving sinners who do not repent of their sins. This would be to deny himself and act contrary to his word. But nothing can stand in the way of his sovereign, irresistible, almighty power to save those who are repentant. "All authority has been given to me in heaven and on earth", and he will use this power to give certain salvation to all who come to him (Matthew 28:18). He said: "All that the

Father gives me will come to me, and the one who comes to me I will by no means cast out" (John 6:37).

7. Think deeply about the infinitely wise and gracious God whose purpose is that his mercy, love, grace, goodness, righteousness, wisdom and power should be in Christ for the salvation of those who believe. Therefore, whoever comes to Christ by faith is, by that act, honouring God. There is more glory given to God by our coming to Christ by faith than if we could keep the whole law. Do not deceive yourselves into thinking that it is a matter of little importance whether you come to Christ or not. Your refusal to do so is as great an act of hatred against God as your nature is capable of.

8. Consider how, by your coming to Christ, he will become yours in a closer relationship than your wife, your husband or your children. Christ is nearer to believers than any natural relations can be. And that means that the glory of Christ is yours when you come to him. Is it a small thing in your eyes that Christ could be yours? Is it nothing to you that all his glory and eternal blessedness could be yours?

9. "How shall we escape if we neglect so great a salvation?" (Hebrews 2:3). Unbelievers who do not repent when they hear the preaching of the gospel are the most evil and ungrateful of all God's creatures. The devils themselves, as wicked as they are, are not guilty of this sin, for they have never had the opportunity of receiving salvation.

Someone may say: "What shall we do, then?" Take the advice of the apostle: "Today . . . hear his voice, do not harden your hearts" (Hebrews 3:7, 8). "Now is the accepted time; behold now is the day of salvation" (II Corinthians 6:2). This is as good a time to make certain of your salvation as any time you are ever likely to have in this world. Christ has waited long for you and who knows how soon he may leave you to yourself and then you will never find him?

Unbelief is often disguised in other attitudes of mind, such as the following:

i. Some say: "We believe the word that is preached as far as we can. We do many things willingly and are careful not to do wrong. What more is required of us?" Thinking they have done their duty, they ask the question the people asked Jesus in John 6:28: "What shall we do, that we may work the works of God?" Simon Magus heard the word and believed as well as he could. Herod heard John's preaching. But neither were true believers. Such actions as these can all be done by unbelievers. All sorts of hypocrites perform many duties without possessing true faith. Their unbelief is disguised by all their activity.

There is one special act of faith whereby you yield willing obedience to God in everything. This special act is accompanied by a change that affects the whole nature. "If anyone is in Christ, he is a new creature; old things have passed away; behold, all things have become new" (II Corinthians 5:17). Without this basic act of faith, all other actions are no evidence that a person is a believer.

ii. Some say they have tried coming to Christ and believing on him but they seem to make no progress. They secretly despair of ever receiving him as set out in the gospel. I would ask these people to remember the disciples who were fishing all night but caught nothing (see Luke 5:3—6). Christ comes to them and tells them to let down their nets once more. Peter reminds the Lord how they had worked all night in vain but at the Master's word he lets down the net and the net broke because of the great number of fish caught. Have you become tired and disappointed in your efforts to come to Christ? Try once more — you do not know what success he may give you.

It is not your failures but the giving up of your attempts to come to Christ that will be your ruin. Think of the woman of Canaan in Matthew 15:22–28. At first Christ did not answer her. Then the disciples asked him to send her away. Moreover Jesus said he was only sent to those who were Israelites. But she did not give up but worshipped Jesus and said: "Lord, help me". He then likened her to the dogs which were not to have children's bread given to them. If she had given up now, she would never have obtained mercy. But she would not take "no" for an answer until she was given her request. It may be you have prayed many times without success, as you think. Do not give up. "Blessed is the man who listens to me, watching daily at my gates, waiting at the posts of my doors" (Proverbs 8:34). "Let us pursue the knowledge of the Lord" (Hosea 6:3).

iii. Some say that they know they must come to Christ and believe on him or they are lost, but they are too busy at present and there will be time enough to think seriously about this later on. Can anything be more foolish than to consider the trifling things of the present more than the happiness or misery of an eternal state? You come to hear the word, and the language of your heart is: "A little sleep, a little slumber, a little folding of the hands to sleep" (Proverbs 6:10). Deceived in this way, thousands perish every day. Satan's greatest success is in making people think they have plenty of time before they die to consider their eternal welfare. Remember, scripture limits you to the present day, without any certainty that you will have another day in which to receive grace and mercy (see II Corinthians 6:2; Hebrews 3:7, 13).

iv. Some find so much satisfaction in their present sinful pleasures that they cannot part with them. If you are like this, we must speak plainly and leave you in no doubt that you cannot expect mercy if your heart is still clinging even to one sin. Of course you will not be perfectly free from the sinfulness of your old nature when you become a true believer. But you must love either God or the world, Christ or Satan, holiness or sin. There is no third choice (see II Corinthians 6:15—18). With regard to your supposed pleasures, unless you are in Christ you have never had any real pleasure. A few moments of the joys to be found in him are far better than the longest time spent in the unbelieving pleasures of this world upon which God's curse rests (see Proverbs 3:13—18).

v. There are those who say that some Christian believers they know are no better than themselves and, therefore, they too should be regarded as Christians. I say to them that there are those who call themselves Christians who are false, pretending to be what they are not. But they will have to bear their own judgment. It is also a sad fact that some true believers are careless in the way they live and so displease God and dishonour Christ and the gospel. But these are not the people for you to copy.

The world cannot make a right judgment of believers. Only the spiritual person discerns the things of God (see I Corinthians 2:14). The faults and failings of the godly are seen by everyone but their graces are often unseen. "The royal daughter is all glorious within" (Psalm 45:13). When you are able to make a right judgment of other true believers, you will want nothing better than to be in their company (see Psalm 16:3).

16.
How Christians may find fresh grace to renew their spiritual life

Rivers become wider and deeper as they get near the ocean; so grace ought to flow more fully and freely in believers as they draw nearer to heaven. As they get nearer to eternity, believers long to have their backslidings healed and their failures forgiven. They desire a fresh activity of divine grace to make them more fruitful and holy, to the praise of God and the increase of their own peace and joy. They want to know that though their "outward man is perishing, yet the inward man is being renewed day by day" (II Corinthians 4:16). The glory of kings is in the wealth and peace of their subjects; so the glory of Christ is in the grace and holiness of his subjects. In Psalm 92:12—15 the psalmist says: "The righteous shall flourish like a palm tree, he shall grow like a cedar in Lebanon. Those who are planted in the house of the Lord shall flourish in the courts of our God. They shall still bear fruit in old age; they shall be fresh and flourishing, to declare that the Lord is upright; he is my rock, and there is no unrighteousness in him".

The palm tree is more beautiful and fruitful and the cedar has a longer life than any other tree. So the righteous are compared to these trees but through sinful neglect many Christians are more like shrubs in the desert. Unless we are planted in the house of the Lord, we cannot flourish. Do not let us deceive ourselves. We may belong to a church, but unless we are rooted and built up in Christ Jesus, we shall not flourish in grace and fruitfulness (Colossians 2:7). When believers are living in Christ they receive a continual supply of heavenly food which keeps them strong and healthy. The fruit of holy obedience is seen in them. This makes their life appear attractive to others. Blessed be God for the good word of his grace which encourages us when we feel the deadness and temptations of old age. Nothing but the faithfulness and power of God can keep us to the end.

I want to finish with the following four points:

1. The nature of spiritual life is normally to grow and increase to the end. There is a temporary faith which withers and fades away. This is described by our Lord Jesus Christ: "He who received the seed on stony places, this is he who hears the word and immediately receives it with joy; yet he has no root in himself but endures only for a while" (Matthew 13:20, 21). True faith, however, is described in Proverbs 4:18: "The path of the just is like the shining sun that shines ever brighter unto the perfect day". The light of the morning looks very much the same as the light of the evening. The difference is that one goes on to give more light until it comes to perfection, and the other gradually becomes darker until it is midnight. So there is a difference between the true believer and one who has no spiritual life in him. Where there is saving grace, it will continue growing to the end. Sometimes there may be a period when the soul seems to be slipping back rather than going forward. Then the grace of God will give it no rest until it recovers and starts growing again. Those who are not real believers are deceived by their own souls and make no effort to recover themselves from the eternal ruin ahead of them. Sometimes, when he is converted, the believer is in great darkness and trouble because of Satan's temptations. But the grace which

79

he has received as the morning light continues to increase, in spite of the clouds and darkness.

Spiritual life is also like living water, an unfailing well of water springing up into everlasting life (see John 4:10, 14). A pond, however large, may dry up completely in time of drought. So, too, the life of many who call themselves Christians, dries up when they come into trouble or temptation. The spiritual life in a true believer can never fail but continues to spring up.

The promises of God were the means by which we first believed. It is also by these precious promises that the divine nature is kept alive in us (see II Peter 1:4). Let us look at just one promise: "For I will pour water on him who is thirsty and floods on the dry ground; I will pour my Spirit on your descendants and my blessing on your offspring; they will spring up among the grass like willows by the water courses" (Isaiah 44:3, 4). This is not only a promise to the Jews but also to the church of Jesus Christ. In ourselves we are thirsty and dry ground, bearing no fruit. But then God pours out the water of his Spirit and the blessing of his grace and we grow, under the influence of the promises, like a tree by a stream.

With regard to the grace given at conversion to the chosen people of God under the new covenant, this is absolutely free and without any conditions attached. But there are conditions connected with the promises by which believers grow in grace. A careful obedience to the gospel is expected from us in order that we may become spiritually fruitful (see II Peter 1:4–10). The chief difference between the glory and beauty of the church seen in the promises of the gospel, and the life of the church seen in professing Christians, is that they do not fulfil these conditions.

God has provided food for our spiritual life to grow and become strong. This is the word of God (see

I Peter 2:2, 3). If we do not eat our daily food, we become weak and useless. So we must value and feed on the good word of God's grace, which is able to keep our spiritual life healthy and growing, even in old age.

2. Believers are liable to temptations and to grow tired in their spiritual life. But a true believer will always know when he is suffering from some spiritual disease and will long for a quick recovery. It is the sad experience of all believers in all the churches in the world that a general weakening of spiritual life causes the loss of their first faith, love and works. This was true of the churches in Asia to whom John wrote the letters in Revelation 2 and 3.

There is also the sudden temptation which brings great spiritual distress. David refers to such an occasion in Psalm 38. He felt he had departed from God and had foolishly continued in that sinful state instead of seeking mercy. He had a continual sense of God's displeasure and longed to be brought out from that miserable condition. We may not fall so low as David, but to whatever degree we sin, the heart will know its own bitterness (see Proverbs 14:10). Many things cause a gradual loss of spiritual life and power. We become so used to the forms of public worship and private devotion that they begin to lose their meaning. We can be too occupied with the affairs and pleasures of this life, and do not put to death the sins which are so naturally attractive to us.

3. Many who call themselves Christians no longer enjoy the life and fruitfulness resulting from belief in the promises of God. They need to be stirred up to know they are sick and to seek a cure. Many believers have given way to laziness, neglect or some other temptation. David knew what it was and expressed his joy at having been restored in Psalm 103:1—5. God has given great warnings of the danger of wasting

away spiritually and has made great promises to enable us to recover. If you do not know anything about such experiences, it may be because your soul has never been in a strong and healthy state. Anyone who has been weak and ill all his life does not know what it is to be healthy and strong. There are some who live in all kinds of sin. If you talk to them about their evil ways and their need to be restored, they will treat you as Lot was treated by his sons-in-law. "But to his sons-in-law he seemed to be joking" (Genesis 19:14). Such people should ask themselves whether they have known anything at all of the grace of God. Or it may be you are asleep in a false sense of your own security. You are like the church at Laodicea which said it had "need of nothing" and did not know it was "wretched, miserable, poor, blind, and naked" (Revelation 3:17). Like Ephraim, you have grey hairs and are in a dying condition but you "do not return to the Lord (your) God, nor seek him for all this" (Hosea 7:9, 10). You are like those whom Christ called "the well", who "have no need of a physician". But he "did not come to call the righteous, but sinners, to repentance" (Mark 2:17).

Could it be said of many of us that we have become tired of God, like his people of old? "You have been weary of me, O Israel" (Isaiah 43:22). There is often a failure to keep up regular family prayer, and little real desire to attend divine worship. But even where such duties are regularly carried out, there is a weariness in which we may draw near to God with our lips when our hearts are far from him (see Matthew 15:8). We have a great need to watch and pray. A thousand things in the ordinary business of life, resulting in a natural tiredness, prevent us from stirring up all the grace God has given us. And especially any sin we do not deal with in our lives will make worship seem a tiresome burden.

Those things which bring most glory to God are humility, a real sorrow for sin, an eager willingness and delight in the ways of God, love and self-denial. Are we being fruitful in these things, even in old age? (see II Peter 1:8). We can test ourselves in the following way.

i. Do we have a good spiritual appetite for the word of God and an experience of the grace of God? Some people hear the preaching merely in order to have their own ideas confirmed. Others go to pass judgment on the preacher. Only a few prepare themselves to receive the word of God into their hearts. As we grow older we lose much of our natural appetite for food. We say it does not taste as good as when we were younger. But the change is in ourselves, not in the food. So it is with the word of God which the Psalmist says is sweeter than honey and the honeycomb (Psalm 19:10). If we were hungry, we would find a sweetness in its bitterest reproofs.

ii. Do we make religion our chief concern in life? With many of us, everything else is put before the one essential thing — our spiritual welfare. If we are continually occupied with the affairs of the world and only just make time now and then to consider spiritual realities, it is a sure sign that our spiritual life is wasting away. When that happens we lack love for other Christians and are unwilling to respond to the calls of God to repent and amend our ways.

4. There is a way back to spiritual strength and fruitfulness, even in old age.

i. No-one is without hope, even if fallen to a low level, but we must use the right means to recover. Trees which have grown old or unfruitful are given new life by digging around them and fertilising them. They are not taken up and planted somewhere else. Some professing believers have turned to false religions for help and have withered and died. If they had used the proper means for their healing they might have lived.

ii. Sinful acts will have to be put to death and all the teaching of Christ carefully obeyed. We must not, of course, fall into the error of the Pharisees. Confessions, pilgrimages, fasts and the repetition of many prayers do not make us acceptable to God. There must be a redoubling of effort to put away sin. It is also absolutely necessary to read the scriptures regularly (or hear them read), to hear the word of God preached and to watch and pray against temptation. So the mind will be kept spiritual and heavenly in its thoughts and affections. All these things, however, cannot be done in our own strength. We are not "sufficient of ourselves to think anything as being from ourselves, but our sufficiency is of God" (II Corinthians 3:5). Faith must obtain the help of Christ in whatever efforts we try to make. Without faith they will be useless and rejected by God.

iii. The restoration of believers who have lost their spiritual health and strength is an act of sovereign grace, the work of Almighty God whose grace and love no-one can resist. God has provided great and precious promises which we are to make use of for this purpose. Let us look at some of these promises in Hosea 14:

Verse 1: The true Israel of God, his chosen people, were affected by the sins of the whole nation. Hosea had earlier pronounced dreadful judgments on the nation for their great wickedness. But nothing can prevent the almighty power of God doing by his grace what he chooses with his people. God was still "the Lord your God", and though they had fallen they were graciously invited to return.

Verse 2: God by his prophet shows the people how they ought to be praying: "Take away all iniquity and receive us graciously". No sin is left out. When the pardon of all sin has been obtained and the people begin to feel the love of God once more, there is the longing to know that God has freely accepted them and that they are no longer under his displeasure.

Verse 3: God expects a full and free confession of the two great sins which ruined his people — confidence in man, and false worship. "Assyria shall not save us, we will not . . . say any more to the work of our hands, You are our gods: for in you the fatherless find mercy".

Verse 4: Although God will heal our backslidings and love us freely, yet we are required to repent, and he gives us the grace to do so. God gives himself the title: "I am the Lord who heals you" (Exodus 15:26). The only reason for healing us is his free, undeserved love. His healing includes the pardon of past sin and the supply of grace to make us fruitful in obedience. "I will be like the dew to Israel" (verse 5).

It is a truly great thing to have our backslidings healed and to have a sense of the beauty and glory of God's love, mercy and grace at work in our lives again. Do not despair of receiving such fresh springs of grace. Obtain them by faith in God's promises, as they are offered through Jesus Christ, the glorious mediator.

All our supplies of grace come from Jesus Christ and from him alone. "Without me you can do nothing". "I have been crucified with Christ; it is no longer I who live, but Christ lives in me; and the life which I now live in the flesh I live by faith in the Son of God, who loved me, and gave himself for me". (John 15:5; Galatians 2:20). The only way of receiving supplies of spiritual strength and grace from him is by faith. He lives in our hearts by faith, he acts in us by faith, and we live by faith in the Son of God. There is only one way to be revived and healed from our backslidings so that we may become fruitful even in old age. We must take a steady look at the glory of Christ in his special character, in his grace and work, as shown to us in the scripture. In Psalm 34:5 David says: "They looked to him and were radiant, and their faces were not ashamed". Their faith was seen in their looking to him, that is, to Christ, or the glory of God in him. Their act of trust arose from a consideration of who and what he is. They were refreshed by the spiritual, saving, light received from him. So may we, as we look with the same faith to the same Jesus Christ. "Look to me, and be saved, all you ends of the earth" (Isaiah 45:22). Our whole salvation, including everything in our spiritual life, depends on this look. This is the way we receive grace and glory. "Therefore I will look to the Lord; I will wait for the God of my salvation; my God will hear me" (Micah 7:7).

A continual view of the glory of Christ will have the blessed effect of changing us more and more into the likeness of Christ. Perhaps other ways and means have failed to make us Christlike. Let us put this way to the test.

Most of our spiritual weakness and unfruitfulness is caused by letting other things occupy our minds too easily. When we have our minds filled with Christ and his glory, and our hearts burn with great love to him, we shall have no room for any other things (see Colossians 3:1—5). It is only a continual view of Christ and his glory that will stir us up and encourage us to watch and fight continually against the deceitful workings of sin. The experience of those things which make Christ glorious has a power to make us want to do only those things that please him.

Other volumes in the
**Great Christian Classics
Series**

No.4 BY GOD'S GRACE ALONE
Prepared by H.J.Appleby
Abraham Booth's **The Reign of Grace.**
Paperback, 73 pages. ISBN 0 946462 01 1.
"One does not doubt that Mr Appleby has made a sound job of this rendering..."

Gospel Magazine

No.5 BORN SLAVES
Prepared by Clifford Pond
Martin Luther's **The Bondage of the Will.**
Paperback, 93 pages. ISBN 0 946462 02 X.
"This excellent, easy to read edition of Luther's book will help us to think clearly about a subject which has often been the source of such confusion."

Fellowship Magazine

No.6 THE GLORY OF CHRIST
Prepared by H.Mockford
John Owen's **The Glory of Christ.**
Paperback, 86 pages. ISBN 0 946462 13 5.

No.7 CHRISTIANS ARE FOR EVER
Prepared by H.Lawrence
John Owen's **The Perseverance of the Saints.**
Paperback, 84 pages. ISBN 0 946462 14 3.

GREAT CHRISTIAN CLASSICS SERIES:

Easier-to-read and abridged versions of Christian classics.

No.1 LIFE BY HIS DEATH

Prepared by H.J.Appleby
John Owen's **The Death of Death in the Death of Christ.**
Paperback, 87 pages. ISBN 0 9505476 3 8.
"...a brilliant abridgement. The whole church of Christ stands in debt to John Appleby for undertaking this work."

Stuart Olyott

No.2 GOD WILLING

Prepared by H.Mockford
John Flavel's **Divine Conduct or The Mystery of Providence.**
Paperback, 65 pages. ISBN 0 9505476 6 2.
"This volume borders on the masterly...You must buy it and read it again and again."

Evangelical Magazine of Wales

No.3 BIBLICAL CHRISTIANITY

Prepared by B.R.Woods
John Calvin's **The Institutes of the Christian Religion.**
Paperback, 125 pages. ISBN 0 9505476 7 0.
"This is an excellent little book. It deserves a worldwide circulation!"

Evangelical Times